Maury W Donaho

Mary Donoho, circa 1859. She was about fifty years old. From a tintype less than two by three inches. Photo courtesy Elma Cornelius McWhorter.

Mary Donoho

New First Lady
of the
Santa Fe Trail

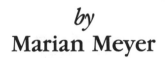

by
Marian Meyer

foreword by
Marc Simmons

Ancient City Press
Santa Fe, New Mexico

International Standard Book Number:
0-941270-70-X clothbound
0-941270-69-6 paperback

Library of Congress Catalog Number:
90-056218

Book and cover design by Mary Powell

Page i: the signature of Mary Donoho from a 1849
probate document.

Cover Painting
Dream of the West
By Roy Grinnell
Member of the Cowboy Artists of America
Private Collection of Ike Kalangis
Model Kristin Kalangis Malmstrom

Library of Congress Cataloging-in-Publication Data

Meyer, Marian, 1927-
    Mary Donoho : new first lady of the Santa Fe Trail / by
Marian ; foreword, Marc Simmons. — 1st ed.
        p.   cm.
    Includes bibliographical references (p.   ) and index.
    ISBN 0-941270-70-X (clothbound) : — ISBN 0-941270-69-6
(pbk.) :
        1. Donoho, Mary, 1807-1880. 2. Women pioneers — Southwest,
New — Biography. 3. Pioneers — Southwest, New — Biography.
4. Southwest, New — Biography. I. Title.
    F786.D666   1991
979'.02'092 — dc20
    [B]   90-56218
                                                              CIP
    10 9 8 7 6 5 4 3

To
Lee

Contents

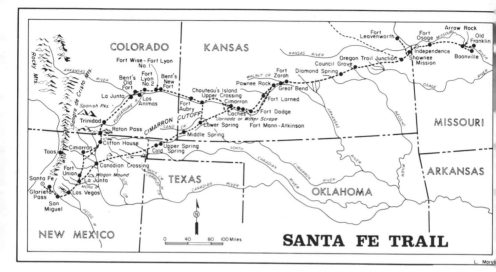

Santa Fe Trail. From Larry M. Beachum, William Becknell: Father of the Santa Fe Trade *(El Paso: Texas Western Press, 1982). Used with permission.*

Foreword

by Marc Simmons

Like many subjects related to the history of the American West, the story of the Santa Fe Trail continues to engage the interest and fire the imagination of a large audience. And no wonder, for during the six decades that comprise the annals of the the trail, 1821 to 1880, there can be found some of the most dramatic events ever to occur on the far western frontier. The very name "Santa Fe Trail" has come to symbolize romance, adventure, tragedy, and triumph, the very themes in the theater of human experience that play best on history's stage.

During the last several years, enthusiasm for the trail has ballooned. In 1987 it became a National Historic Trail under jurisdiction of the National Park Service, a promotion in status that was highly newsworthy. A number of recent historic preservation projects along the pioneer route have also attracted attention. A national organization, the Santa Fe Trail Association, was formed in 1986 and in a short time has taken the lead in promotional and historical endeavors. Researchers and writers have been led to examine neglected facets of the trail's story and to publish a long list of authoritative books that provide fresh insights and attract still more interest in the subject.

Marian Meyer now joins the ranks of those authors with her carefully researched biography of Mary Dodson Donoho, whom she aptly describes as "the new first lady of the Santa Fe Trail." Until Mrs. Meyer discovered, almost by accident, that Mary Donoho had come over the trail in 1833 and had remained in Santa Fe until 1837, her presence in New Mexico had not even been suspected. Indeed, before they had learned the full details, some historians were heard to remark that it couldn't possibly be so, because with all the archival work done by previous scholars her name would surely have surfaced before now.

Yet, there it was, beyond any shadow of doubt: Mary Donoho and her husband William had crossed the trail from Missouri in the 1830s, became innkeepers at Santa Fe for four years, had two more children, and then returned east in a wagon caravan. By diligent digging, Marian Meyer had at last brought the outline of that buried story to light. And she did more. Combing archives in Missouri, she pieced together Mary Donoho's early history, before the start of her Santa Fe Trail adventure. Meyer also followed the Donoho track to east Texas and the town of Clarksville, just below the Red River, where the couple passed the last part of their lives, again as hoteliers. By a curious coincidence, Mary Donoho died in 1880, the very year the railroad reached New Mexico's capital and the Santa Fe Trail closed.

Assembling this narrative from scattered fragments has not been an easy task. Mary Donoho, so far as is known, kept no diary or trail journal, so that whatever she may have experienced in her overland travels is lost to us. Likewise, the nature of her life and work while at Santa Fe remains almost a total blank. The author has done a commendable job of shading in these gaps with historically sound and restrained speculations. Unless some new body of documentation suddenly appears, it seems doubtful that anyone will ever be able to do more.

Hezekiah Brake, who made his own trail crossing in 1858, wrote in his published account: "In those days the women dreaded worse than death, the perils of the Western trails." That being the case, it may help explain why so few women dared set out on the trail to Santa Fe, especially prior to 1846 when its dangers were most acute. That Mary Donoho willingly undertook the trip suggests she was a lady of uncommon courage. Events of her later life, about which information is available, would seem to confirm that assumption.

Mary Donoho's story and Marian Meyer's efforts to bring it to light form the contents of this book. All those who cherish the memory of the historic old Santa Fe Trail will value the result and will delight in adding this volume to their collections of trail literature. Mary Donoho, we can guess, would have been sincerely pleased.

Acknowledgements

This book is the result of the assistance of many individuals who either love history or were excited about the discovery of Mary Donoho, and wanted to help. I am pleased to acknowledge them here.

My friend Sherry Smith, former Chief Archivist at the New Mexico State Records Center and Archives, averred from the very beginning that Mary Donoho's discovery was significant enough to change a bit of Santa Fe Trail history. She accompanied me on the first two research trips and has been available throughout the project for discussion, advice and leaning on.

On the day he first saw the documentation of Mary Donoho, Marc Simmons said a book must be written about her. I had only gotten as far as thinking she would be the first chapter in a book I was planning on pioneer Santa Fe women. Marc said she was far too important for that. He has been supportive throughout the writing of the book and I am indebted to him.

I am continually amazed at how helpful librarians and archivists at most research facilities tend to be. Rarely does one encounter indifference. Some of them have become my personal friends over the years. Among those who offered assistance in the preparation of this book were New Mexico State Library staff members Ingrid Volnhofer, Kathleen Schumpert, Norma McCallan, Nancy Fischer, Peggy Medina Giltrow, Betty Sena and Robert Upton. I am particularly indebted to Ingrid and Robert who helped me find innumerable out-of-state resources.

At the Museum of New Mexico, History Library *jefe* Orlando Romero was in on the discovery of Mary Donoho from the first day and has shared some of the triumphs and disappointments of the research. He was ever helpful. In the Photo Archives of the museum Dr. Richard Rudisill, Photo Historian, and Arthur Olivas, Photo Archivist, searched out the oldest photographs of Santa Fe and the Exchange Hotel. While in Palestine, Texas, I called Arthur who advised me on how to have the photographer reproduce the little tintype of Mary Donoho. He said emphatically, "No restoration!" Dick Rudisill later studied the photograph and assessed its probable date.

At the New Mexico State Records Center and Archives, the late Kay Dorman helped me find the only known reference to William Donoho in their holdings. Chief Archivist Richard Salazar and Al Regensberg were always willing to help in research questions and Arlene Padilla cheerfully photocopied materials.

Other Santa Feans who gave assistance were Dr. Myra Ellen Jenkins, Linda Tigges, Dr. Stanley M. Hordes, Thomas B. Catron III and Samuel Ballen, owner of the La Fonda Hotel.

In Albuquerque the staff at both the Library of Latter Day Saints and University of New Mexico Special Collections were helpful when I was searching out census records or old books. Ann Mossman of the New Mexico Genealogical Society contributed information. In Columbia at the State Historical Society of Missouri, Manuscript Specialist Sharon Fleming was helpful, as was Reference Specialist Laurel Boeckman. I am also indebted to my husband's cousin, Dr. Dallas Meyer, Professor Emeritus of the University of Missouri, for an orientation of the campus and for courtesies extended to Sherry and me by him and his wife, Louise. In the Camden County Courthouse, Virginia Morgan was most hospitable in providing a map and precise instructions for finding the Glaize City Cemetery. Margot Swovelan at Kansas State Historical Society also gave assistance.

I have not yet met Fern Moreland of Camdenton, Missouri, longtime editor of the *Camden County Historian*, but our correspondence has been voluminous. She provided much background material on the Dodsons and made a special trip to the Waynesville County Courthouse to find the 1839 Dodson probate document for me. My heartfelt thanks. Martha Hoffman of the Pulaski County Historical Society, Waynesville, Missouri, sent information and a photograph. Dr. Leo E. Oliva of Woodston, Kansas, provided information in preparation for my trip to the National Archives, where William Lind assisted in my search. At the University of Texas in Austin, in the Eugene Barker Texas History Center, Ralph Elder and William Richter were extremely helpful in my research of the

John Henry Brown Papers, and in suggesting other sources. From Southern Methodist University in Dallas came assistance from Dr. David J. Weber, Dedman Professor of History and Research Assistant Jane Lenz Elder. Tom Amoscato, Reference Librarian at Corpus Christi State University, was also helpful.

Clarksville, Texas, was the hotbed of resource material for Mary Donoho. Without the assistance of the good people there, we might not have had a Mary Donoho book. Their hospitality in preparing luncheons for us on two different occasions was above and beyond the courtesies generally extended to researchers. The list is long: Mary Kate Hale, volunteer librarian and ramrod of the committee who met with us; Mary Hausler, Red River County Clerk and her staff; Librarian La Wana Byers of the Red River County Library; Anne Evetts, the gourmet cook of the two luncheons, who also made arrangements with Sharon Wallace, a Clarksville photographer, who volunteered to duplicate the Clarksville Historical Society photographs for the book. Anne is the great-granddaughter of Eugene Bowers, another longtime county clerk, author and collector of historic material. Anne is the family custodian of the Bowers Papers and offered an unpublished sketch written by him for use in the book. Other members of the Clarksville Historical Society who contributed information were Anne's mother, Josephine Russell, Ruth McCulloch, Mr. and Mrs. Pat C. Beadle, Susan Hughston and Jim Clark, great-great-grandson of the founder of Clarksville.

Others who gave assistance were Milan Hughston of the Amon Carter Museum, Fort Worth; David Haynes, Institute of Texas Cultures, San Antonio; Barbara Marine, Director, Washington Public Library, Washington, Illinois; and Caryl S. Scott of the N. H. Scott & Hebblethwaite Funeral Home, Glenview, Illinois.

And of course, in Palestine, Texas, there is the inestimable lady, Elma Cornelius McWhorter, who put the icing on the cake when she provided the little tintype of Mary Donoho. The only living great-grandchild of the Donoho's, she related valuable reminiscences. In January 1991, when the editing process on the book was almost complete, Mrs. McWhorter's husband died following a long illness. With unaccustomed time on her hands, she started searching through the family papers, finding two long-forgotten tintypes of Mary Donoho's daughters, as well as old letters and other memorabilia. She shipped two boxes to me. So, at the eleventh hour, the material was examined and incorporated into the book. I was delighted that it was found in time and thank her for entrusting her precious family heirlooms to me.

Raymond E. Cornelius, Jr., of Lufkin, Texas, a Donoho great-great-grandson, was most helpful in getting the tintype reproduced and in recalling important information. He also found a valuable family document late in the game which was used in the book.

Special thanks are due those who made possible the use of the painting which appears on the cover of this book. Owner of the portrait, Ike Kalangis, is the father of the model, Kristin Kalangis Malmstrom, who, like Mary Donoho, has red hair. "Dream of the West" was painted by Santa Fe artist Roy Grinnell, who is widely recognized for the uncompromised historical accuracy of his work. His wife Peggy made available the transparency of the painting.

Lastly, I thank my husband Lee for the thousands of miles he drove in search of Mary Donoho.

Prologue

The story of how Mary Donoho was found is almost as interesting as the story itself. One does not often have the opportunity to start out with a totally unknown subject and end up with enough information to write a good and proper book. The notation which led to her discovery sat for three years in a box on my worktable, without my ever having laid eyes on the story it told.

In 1984, while researching old issues of *The Santa Fe New Mexican* on microfilm, a headline caught my eye. It said, "First White Child Born in New Mexico," but I could not read the article itself because the small print was blurred. I made a notation on a card and planned to look it up later at another library, but instead it got tossed into my box labeled, "Things to do When I Have Time." It lay there forgotten until I discovered it three years later while searching for something else. By that time I was working on a Santa Fe pioneer women series and decided to check it out in case it had something I could use.

On 5 May 1987, when I looked it up again at the State Library, I remembered that the blurred print was why I had not been able to read it the first time. So over to the History Library at the Museum of New Mexico I went, hoping I could cajole Orlando Romero, the librarian, into letting me see the original newspaper. He is very protective of those old fragile issues and only lets them be used as a last resort. He suggested I check their film first since it might be a better run. It was.

As I read the article, the hair on the back of my neck stood up. Dated 19 August 1885, it told that James Donoho, a wealthy hotel and cattle man from Clarksville, Texas, born in Santa Fe in 1837, was visiting his birthplace. It described how his mother, father and sister had crossed over the historic Santa Fe Trail in 1833 with one hundred-fifty Missouri adventurers. The couple had lived in Santa Fe several years, ran a hotel and had two more children there. Furthermore, when they returned to Missouri, they took with them three Texas women who had been Indian captives, rescued by Donoho's father.

I rushed out of the film room to find Orlando. With him was Ingrid Vollnhofer, a librarian from the State Library. They both came into the film room and looked the story over. Imperturbable Ingrid reacted in her usual calm manner. Orlando is more excitable. He knows his history and takes it very seriously. This contradicted everything he knew. He practically shouted, "That's impossible! There weren't any Anglo women in Santa Fe in the 1830s! Why, that was during the Albino Perez rebellion!" After things calmed down a little, we discussed whether the story could be a hoax, way back in 1885. Still, we agreed that if it were true, one of the plums of research had fallen neatly into my lap. It meant that a United States woman had traveled the Santa Fe Trail thirteen years before Susan Shelby Magoffin's well known journey and could very well displace her as the First Lady of the Santa Fe Trail.

Sometime later, out of curiosity, I checked the old newspaper name file at the History Library. Both Harriet and James Donoho were listed. The notation reads: "First Anglo Child Born in New Mexico," instead of "white child." Evidently by the 1930s the Works Progress Administration workers who began the files were using the term "Anglo" instead of "white." Orlando and I were both astonished that the listings had been there for probably fifty years and no researcher had shown any interest in them.

In the beginning all there was to go on were the names James and Harriet Donoho and Clarksville, Texas. I knew that if I could in any way verify the presence of the Donohos in Santa Fe, it would be worth pursuing. The first breakthrough came within two weeks. The little Mormon library in Albuquerque happened to have a census of Red River County, Texas, and James Donoho was on it, with his birthplace listed as New Mexico. Fortunately, that particular census was found first; two others located later said he was born in Mexico. Technically, that was correct; it was Mexican territory. But the discovery meant his parents were in New Mexico in 1837. Also, an inquiry to the Red River County Library in Clarksville brought a reply that, although now gone, the Donohos had indeed been an important family there, and had run the Donoho Hotel for over half a century. In addition, Clarksville and Red River County histories confirmed that the Donohos had lived in Santa Fe in the 1830s.

It was enough corroboration and invited total pursuit of the story. The search has taken me to Texas four times, including Clarksville twice, Austin and Palestine, as well as to Missouri twice. In the beginning the research moved rapidly. Twenty-five days after the original story was found, an archivist friend and I visited Clarksville. I have never before encountered such cordial hospitality while doing research. Mary Kate Hale, a volunteer librarian there, knew we were coming and arranged a wonderful small town welcome for us, with a luncheon to meet members of the Clarksville Historical Society, the county clerk and an articulate ninety-seven year-old lady who had known James Donoho's daughters. In talking to the local residents, we got a feel for the town and learned how strongly they feel about their history. There was a photograph of the Donoho Hotel and we found that Donoho headstones abound in the beautiful old Clarksville Cemetery. My friend Sherry Smith is a skill-ed researcher and in two grueling days we sifted through most of the relevant records in the Red River County Courthouse and Library. We found a treasure-trove of information on the last forty years of Mary Donoho's life.

There was more than enough material to write an article, but before submitting it to my editor, I took it to Marc Simmons, our ultimate Santa Fe Trail authority. As he looked through the infor-mation, his eyes sparkled with excitement. He called it a blockbuster and exclaimed, ''This is great stuff!'' He asked me to write a story for the next issue of *Wagon Tracks*, the newsletter of the Santa Fe Trail Association, and suggested that I plan to write a book on Mary Donoho.

Following the Santa Fe Trail Association Symposium in Hutchin-son, Kansas, in October 1987, Sherry and I went on to Missouri, where we conducted research at the State Historical Society of Missouri in Columbia. We learned that Mary Donoho's family, the Dodsons, were among the earliest pioneers of that state. A con-firmed cemetery tramper, I was not disappointed. We found the little Dodson graveyard, fenced off in a Camden County cornfield, where the ancient tombstones of Mary's parents have stood for a century and a half. A comic episode accompanied that solemn discovery. When we came out of the cemetery my flannel slacks were literally covered with small green Missouri seeds called "sticktights." Sherry's jeans were unaffected and she wouldn't let me back in her Volvo with the sheepskin seats until I changed clothes. After that was accomplished in a small abandoned building nearby, we continued our journey, overcome with laughter.

In December of that year I flew alone to Austin where I suspected some letters written by James Donoho might be in the papers of John Henry Brown, Texas historian. The hunch paid off and Marc Simmons got an exuberant postcard telling of my most significant find to that date. The letters confirmed the story in the *New Mexican* and became the documentation for the Donoho book. Another priceless source in Austin was a listing done in the 1930s by the Works Progress Administration of every person ever mentioned in the *Northern Standard*, Clarksville's newspaper from the 1840s to the 1880s. All the characters in the Donoho drama were there, listed alphabetically. I copied over three hundred entries, with dates and page numbers, to bring home. By borrowing the *Standard* microfilm through the local library, and using the list I was able to go through forty years of newspapers in a relatively short time.

The entire summer of 1988 was filled with fortuitous discoveries. In June after I presented a paper on Mary Donoho for ''Rendezvous 88,'' a seminar at the Santa Fe Trail Center in Larned, Kansas, my husband Lee and I drove on to Clarksville, Texas. I wanted to verify some items and also look again at the Clarksville Historical Society photographs. In 1987 Mary Kate Hale and I had found only a few pictures of questionable quality of the James Donoho home, ''The Cedars.'' This time when she searched their files, she found an additional file folder and the first picture we pulled out was a splendid photograph of James Donoho and his grandson. Several others were equally good of his daughters and son. But alas, there was none of Mary Donoho.

Nevertheless, I was delighted. I had also gotten more information from the probate records of the last Donoho daughter. On the first trip Sherry and I had concentrated on the older Donoho probates. But on this trip I brought home names and addresses of contemporary descendants I had not known existed. They ultimately led me to Elma Cornelius McWhorter. Because William

Cornelius, her grandfather, had been married three times, the odds were that McWhorter was a child of one of the marriages other than the Donoho one. But after writing to her and talking on the telephone, it became apparent that she was indeed the great-granddaughter of Mary Donoho and, miracle of miracles, that she had a picture of her.

Lee and I went to Palestine, Texas, in July. Mrs. McWhorter had also asked her nephew, Raymond E. Cornelius, Jr., the great-great-grandson of Mary Donoho, to be there. It was a dramatic moment. Sitting on the couch in her living room, I opened the ornate tiny tintype and gazed upon the face of Mary Donoho. The object of my fourteen-month search came alive to me at that moment. It was the high point of the Donoho research, made all the more exciting when Ray told me of a large portrait of this same picture which had hung in his father's hotel when he was growing up. He remembered it well and said that Mary Donoho had red hair. My heart leaped at the thought of a picture of her in color, but in the next breath he said it had burned along with the hotel in 1974. We made arrangements at a photo shop to have the tintype copied for the book and of course Marc Simmons got another postcard from me, telling him I had hit the jackpot. I was on a cloud all the way home to Santa Fe.

On the first trip to Columbia, Missouri, time had been severely limited, so a second trip was made to check the Boone County real estate and probate records. A wealth of information was found on property transactions by William and Mary Donoho in the years before they left for Santa Fe.

In between all the traveling, I was doing research in Santa Fe and Albuquerque. I consider Santa Fe to be the most important site in the book, yet I have found less information there than in any of the others. This may change in the future. As Mary Donoho's name becomes familiar to historians, existing bits and pieces of information could become more meaningful. And somewhere, sometime, I believe that an old journal or letter will surface, written by one of the 328 people who traveled in her wagon train. From the 184 members of the caravan or the 144 military men in the escort, some memoir may be waiting to be discovered, buried in an attic trunk or deep in a library collection.

Historians may be surprised to learn that Mary Donoho was not the only woman ahead of Susan Shelby Magoffin on the Santa Fe Trail. Four others also preceded her, making Susan the sixth American woman on the trail instead of the first. The discovery of Mary Donoho may be only the beginning.

Discovering Mary Donoho

Mr. Donoho's father, mother, and an older sister crossed over the historic "Santa Fe Trail" and landed in Santa Fe in the year 1833.
— The Santa Fe New Mexican, 19 August 1885

On 5 May 1987, one hundred-fifty years after the birth of James Donoho in Santa Fe, this century-old story was discovered in *The New Mexican* by the author. It told that forty-eight years after he was born, Donoho returned to the City of the Holy Faith, fulfilling a promise he had made to himself many years earlier to visit the place of his birth. His time in Santa Fe was well chronicled in the newspaper, giving substantial background on the circumstances surrounding his parents' residence in Santa Fe in the 1830s.

Of course, when James Donoho visited Santa Fe, he had no idea that the newspaper record of his visit would prove to be important. He and his family stayed several days in town, visited the areas of interest, then traveled on to Las Vegas where they enjoyed the luxury of the Montezuma Hotel. But his primary goal in Santa Fe was to find the house where he was born and to try to locate any old-timers who had known his father. Apparently he searched alone at first, using former Santa Fe Trail trader Elias Brevoort as an interpreter when he talked to some of the older residents who did not speak

English. Perhaps when that did not succeed he went to the local newspaper.

In those days a town's newspaper offices were frequently not only places where local people congregated, but were also a sort of early chamber of commerce of the town. In 1885 *The New Mexican* office was located in the James Johnson Block on Palace Avenue (where the Catron Building now stands), a few doors west of the Plaza. An ancient photograph shows the entrance to the newspaper offices on the north side.[1]

A photograph shows James Donoho at age sixty-one to be a well-dressed, distinguished looking gentleman with white hair and beard. Thirteen years earlier when he came to Santa Fe he would have looked younger, but with a bearing of wealth and assurance, and, as *The New Mexican* reported, "carrying his age admirably." Apparently the editor who did the interview sensed an important story and was thorough. He elicited enough information for a lengthy article. Headlined "Seeing His Birthplace" with two subheads: "The First White Child Born in New Mexico-A Tale of Early Days," and "A Chatty Interview With a Citizen of Texas Born in Santa Fe in 1837," it began:

> Mr. J. B. Donoho, Clarksville, Texas, is quartered at the Hotel Capital in company with an interesting family consisting of his wife and three children.
>
> This gentleman is a native of Santa Fe, having opened his infant peepers here on the 15th day of May 1837 — nearly half a century ago. In company with about 150 Missouri adventurers, Mr. Donoho's father, mother and an older sister crossed over the historic "Santa Fe trail" and landed in Santa Fe in the year 1833. After disposing of a large quantity of freight which they brought in with them, Mr. Donoho, Sr., engaged in the hotel business on the plaza, and as near as this gentleman can make out, occupied the celebrated "old Fonda" or Exchange hotel as it is now called. In this ancient structure was born Harriet Donoho, in 1835, now dead, but who without doubt was the first white child born in New Mexico. Two years later Mr. J. B. Donoho, the visitor of today, came to gladden the pioneer's household, which makes him the first American child now living born in the territory.[2]

Donoho would not learn until two years later that a few of the details he gave to the editor were incorrect. When he began corresponding with an aunt and uncle on the subject in 1887, he found their version was slightly different. The corrections are shown in brackets below. The remainder of the story was as follows:

The gentleman's father resided here from 1833 to 1839 [1837] and during the latter year returned with his family to Missouri. On this return trip the Senior Donoho carried with him three [two] white women who had been captured on the Texas border [deep in Texas] by Apache [Comanche] Indians and made slaves of. The negotiations for the purchase of these women extended over a period of three months, the Apaches keeping them concealed in the mountain strongholds for fear they would be rescued, and conducting the sale through friendly Mexican traders. Finally a price was agreed upon and the sum of $900 paid the Indians by Mr. Donoho. The women were sent into Santa Fe and tenderly cared for at the Exchange by the family. Upon returning to the Missouri river these women [only one] were provided with means and sent to their respective homes in Texas where they arrived in safety and with hearts overflowing with gratitude for their rescuer and the little band of Missouri pioneers that had aided them. In accordance with a resolve made many years ago Mr. J. B. Donoho, the son, now returns to visit his historic birth-place. It was also one of the greatest desires of his aged mother to visit Santa Fe again, but the wish was never consummated, her death occuring [sic] before the railroad had been extended thus far. During the past few days the gentleman has been employing his time hunting up all the aged people hereabouts, but his efforts to find one, either native or foreign born, who knew his father have been unavailing. He yesterday sought two old time Mexican citizens in hopes of securing the desired result, they informed Mr. Brevoort who acted as interpreter that they were employed in the old Spanish gold mines near Cerrillos at that time; only made brief visits to the city at long intervals, and had little or no acquaintance here. He has faint hopes, however, that Hon. Nicholas Pino, the sage

of Galisteo, will have some recollection of his father and of
himself as a child, and before closing his visit will endeavor
to secure an interview with him.[3] Mr. Donoho is now a
wealthy hotel and cattle man at Clarksville, Texas; carries his
age admirably, and expects to live to see the city of his
nativity one of the greatest inland cities on the continent.[4]

This was met at first reading with skepticism not only by the
author. Was it indeed possible that an Anglo-American woman
was in Santa Fe thirteen years earlier than had previously been
believed? One historian acquaintance dismissed the story with
an adamant and disbelieving, "Oh, you know you can't believe
those old newspaper stories!" So there was much relief when
the first few facts began to confirm the story: James was found
on an 1880 census with his birthplace listed as New Mexico, and
an inquiry brought word from the Red River County Library in
Clarksville, Texas, that the Donohos were indeed an important
part of the town's local history. Historians' contention that no
Anglo-American woman traveled the Santa Fe Trail until 1846,
when Susan Shelby Magoffin made her historic journey on the heels
of General Stephen Watts Kearney and recorded in her journal
the first female impressions of a theretofore completely male
bastion, was no longer true.

As the story unfolded, one fact became abundantly clear:
Mary Donoho eluded historians for one hundred fifty-five years,
simply because so little information on her existed in New Mexico. Sources in Texas yielded an abundance of information on the
last forty years of Mary Donoho's life, but the first thirty remain
sparse and fragmented. There was no Santa Fe newspaper to report
the comings and goings of trail traders in the 1830s; there is no
known journal like Susan Magoffin's to record the hardships and
joys of the Santa Fe Trail; and no letters have been found to Mary's
family in Missouri telling of the birth of another daughter and
a son on the frontier during her four years in Santa Fe.

The search for Mary Donoho ultimately led to the University of
Texas in Austin. There, in the massive collection of the John Henry
Brown Papers, were three letters written by James Donoho to

John Henry Brown, a Texas historian. They provide the undeni-
able — primary source documentation of the Donoho's presence
in Santa Fe in the 1830s. Written on the letterhead of the ''Donoho
House, J. B. Donoho, Proprietor, Clarksville, Texas,'' the three
letters have become the cornerstone of the Mary Donoho story and
are presented below in their entirety:

December 23, 1886

Hol. John H. Brown
Dallas, Texas

Respected Sir:

    I hope you will pardon me the privilege I take in address-
ing you these few lines in search of some early information
in regard to my father who was William Donoho and he
bought three white ladies from the Indians near Santa Fe in
New Mexico, who had been captured on the borders of
Texas. One a Mrs. Plummer who's [sic] family lived
somewhere near Houston. My father returned her to them
and afterwards she wrote a book giving the history of her
capture and life while a prisoner and also her ransom from
Indian captivity by my father. Can you give me any information bearing on the above facts, where I can find a copy of
said book or any of the relatives of Mrs. Plummer's family or
anyone else that can give me any information in regard to
the matter.
    Will be glad to have a copy of your paper with back
numbers giving history of Texas and will send you money for
subscription as soon as I know the amount.
    Trusting to hear from you soon I am with great respect.

Your humble svt.
J. B. Donoho[5]

James' second letter was dated 1 January 1886, but it was 1887.
He simply forgot to change over to the date of the new year.

January 1, 1886

Col. J. H. Brown
Dallas, Texas

Dear Sir:

I accept very gratefully your offer to make mention of any incident of my father's career while in Santa Fe, and will at once put myself in correspondence with my oldest relatives living, for information they can give that I do not possess. My father bought three ladies from the Indians of New Mexico, Mrs. Plummer, Mrs Harris, and Mrs. Horn, all three of whom he brought back to Missouri with him. I have written to the *Texas Farm and Ranch* for several copies of the number containing Chap. 5 of "The Texas Indian Wars" for which I enclosed the money, wishing to distribute them among my relatives. When your book comes from the press, please bear in mind I shall require a dozen copies of the first edition, so speak in time.

Most Sincerely Yours,
J. B. Donoho[6]

The envelope to this letter was saved, and had on it a notation which Brown had written: "Ans. Dec. 25 — sent 'Parker' Chap . . . & asked for more about his father." The *Texas Farm and Ranch* article was the Rachael Parker chapter of his book which would be published in the 1890s, titled *Indian Wars and Pioneers of Texas*. John Henry Brown, historian, soldier, legislator and pioneer citizen of Texas, wrote that book and another important history of Texas, but prior to that, many of the chapters for his books were published first as articles in periodicals and newspapers, which was how James Donoho learned of his work.

Written after he had contacted his aunt and uncle in Missouri for information, the final piece of correspondence between the two men was a seven-page account of James' parents' years in New Mexico. Personal and rich in detail, it opens wide a window on the past.

February 5, 1887

Col. J. H. Brown
Dallas, Texas

Dear Sir:

Since hearing from you last, I have been in correspondence with several parties relative to Mrs. Horn's
book. Not with the success I hoped for, however, but
perhaps you will be able to use what little information I
have gathered.

I mail you at the same time with this, a copy in writing of
Mrs. Horn's book. It was copied as a writing exercise by a
young girl, who afterwards married one of my uncles, B. D.
Dodson of Richland, Missouri. The book is the property of
the girl's mother, a very old lady still living, who cherishes it
as a memento of the daughter who died a number of years
ago. When you have looked it over to your satisfaction, I will
be glad to have you send it back to me in order that I may
return it to the mother of my deceased aunt. My own
mother died in January 1880. Had I supposed that information on these matters would ever have been desirable, I
could have informed myself fully from her, as like Mrs.
Gordon,[7] her memory was a rich storehouse. Accustomed to
hear these things mentioned frequently in the family, I did
not attach much importance to them, until my opportunity
passed away forever.

However, the main incidents are still fresh in the minds of
an uncle and aunt of mine, still living in Missouri, a brother
and sister of my mother's, who had this book sent to me,
together with what they remembered of the incidents as
related by my father and mother, on their return from New
Mexico.

You will observe in Mrs. Horn's recounting her experiences among the Indians, her release from captivity, etc.
She speaks of American traders negotiating for her ransom,
and of Mrs. Harris having left with some who were returning
before her release was effected; of the merchant or traders
having set out for Independence hastily, in consequence of
the war having broken out, etc.

Now I have the testimony of my uncle, Dr. William Dod-

son, and my aunt, Mrs. Lucy Estes, of Camden Co., Mo, that
my father paid out his own money for the purchase of these
three ladies, Mrs. Rachel Plummer, Mrs. Harris and Mrs.
Horn, from the Indians. That Mrs. Plummer and Mrs. Harris were delivered over to him before the breaking out of the
troubles in Santa Fe, and were living there with his family
when compelled to seek safety in flight; that they both
returned to Mo. with my father and mother, and all went to
the home of my grandmother, Mrs. Lucy Dodson of Pulaski
County. After my father accompanied and established them
at my grandmother's, he went back to Santa Fe, to try to
recover what they had in their haste, been compelled to
leave behind in the shape of property, merchandise, mules,
horses, etc. While there this last time, he was able to make
arrangements with some returning traders, to have Mrs.
Horn brought to Mo. Although he had purchased Mrs.
Horn from her captors, he had never seen her, as negotiations had been carried on through Spaniards and friendly
Indians, with whom my father had considerable influence.
Mrs. Horn was left with some friends in Mo. until after the
return of my father the second time, when she came also to
the house of my grandmother, where she saw my father for
the first time, and remained several months. While she was
there at my grandmother's with my mother, my father left
for Texas with Mrs. Plummer, whom he restored to her family, and then went back to Mo. after his own family, consisting of my oldest sister — born in Mo., my second
sister — born in Santa Fe, myself also born in Santa Fe, my
mother, and the slaves she had in the mean time drawn
from the estate of my grandfather, and moved to Texas in
the fall of 1839. Mrs. Harris had relatives in Texas, but
would not return with Mrs. Plummer, so great was her dread
of the Indians. Afterward she learned of some family connections near Boonville, with whom she made her home
until her death soon after. Mrs. Horn lived at my grandmother's several months, but died while on a visit to some
friends in an adjoining county.

Both she and Mrs. Harris did not long survive their
restoration to civilization, as their constitutions had been
completely broken by hardships undergone among the In-

dians, and they bore terrible scars from wounds inflicted by their savage masters. Mrs. Horn's book was written during the interval that elapsed between her arrival in Mo. and my father's second return from Santa Fe, and as she truthfully says, "She did not know to whose noble act she owed her release." But afterward she found out all about it. My relatives attest that they (these restored captives) were ladies in the highest sense of the word. From what I remember hearing from my mother, the ransom of the three cost him about nine hundred dollars in merchandise. He went himself after Mrs. Plummer and Mrs. Harris, and had to carry with him some of my mother's clothes for them to put on, their Indian masters requiring them to give up all they had that was of any service when they gave them into the keeping of the negotiators.

My father spent about five years in Santa Fe, going there in '33 and coming away in '38. He was born in Kentucky in 1798, and died at this place in 1845. He married my mother in Mo. in 1831, my maternal grandfather, Dr. James Dodson having moved there from Tenn. some years previous to that. When my parents decided to make Texas their home, they expected to locate in the vicinity of Austin, but from some cause I do not recollect they settled here, [Clarksville] where the family has since remained, myself being the sole survivor of six children. As it had always been a desire with me to sometime visit the place of my birth, about a year and a half since I, in company with my wife and children, visited Santa Fe, finding no little pleasure in identifying landmarks I had heard my mother speak of though too young when we moved from there to remember anything myself. Had no trouble in locating the home in which I was born, as it cornered on the Plaza, and is now known as the old "Exchange Hotel." My parents liked Santa Fe, and doubtless my father would have spent his life there had it not been for the dangers threatening his family from the turbulent spirit of Mexicans and Indians.

At first I thought of having this little book rewritten, as it is rather difficult to read in places, then it occurred to me that perhaps you would like best to see it as it came from the hands of the child who copied it so many years ago.

Have used my best endeavors to obtain a printed copy, but
without success. My Uncle and Aunt are of great integrity of
character, too conscientious to vary an account in the least,
so that you can rely on these statements which are ''to the
best of their recollections.'' My father was a man of unflag-
ging energy, of great public spirit, and would no doubt have
made his mark high had his career not been cut short by
death at the age of forty-seven years. Of my mother's energy
and commanding spirit, there are too many now living to
bear witness of for me to enter more fully into details.

If my efforts avail the least to furnish you any desirable
material, I shall feel very thankful, or if you can suggest
anything else I can do, will gladly undertake it. With very
best wishes, believe me.

Truly yours,
J. B. Donoho

James then added the following:

I forgot to mention that while in Santa Fe it was settled to
my satisfaction, that my second sister born in 1835, and
myself, born in 1837, were the first white Americans born in
Santa Fe [''New Mexico'' is inserted above Santa Fe]. The
honor or distinction (if it can so be called) had been claimed
by others in behalf of one born there in 1838, but which was
later than my own and sister's.[8]

Mary's four years in Santa Fe were only a small fragment of her
seventy-three years of life but they may have played an important
role in testing her mettle for the years ahead when she would single-
handedly rear her family and run a hotel in Texas. Even though
we know few personal details about Mary Dodson Donoho until
her Texas years, there is no question that she was an intrepid and
extraordinary woman. Along with her parents, she was one of
the earliest pioneers of Camden County, Missouri. Her experiences
in traveling with her family from place to place in Tennessee and
Alabama, then to the wilds of the Ozark country may have honed
a desire in her for travel and new lands, which would lead to her
adventure on the Santa Fe Trail, then back to Missouri and on
to Texas.

Missouri Beginnings

Glaize City, once a thriving community . . . is now identified mainly by a cemetery. Dr. Jim Dodson, one of the county's earliest settlers, was credited with the birth of the town.
— Fern Moreland, *Camden County Historian, 1983*

*M*ary Dodson moved with her family from county to county and state to state many times until her father, Dr. James Dodson, finally decided to settle in Camden County, Missouri. An early history of Camden County details several of those moves and tells of Mary's parent's early life:

James and Lucy (Davis) Dodson, were born in Virginia and Tennessee, respectively, the former's birth occurring about 1772, and his death on the 23rd of December, 1832.[1] When he was about eleven years old he removed to Tennessee with his parents, and located in what is now Sevier County. Here he grew to manhood on a farm, and after his marriage, in 1804, he became a disciple of Aesculapius, and eventually became an eminent physician. From East Tennessee he moved to Middle Tennessee, and located on a branch of Duck River, where he erected a very fine grist-mill, and resided here about eight years. He next took up his abode in Jackson County, Ala., thence, about seven years later to Jefferson County, Tenn., and from there to Hawkins County, and finally to Boone County, MO. He died in Camden County, while on his way with his family to Springfield, but left his wife and children in fairly good circumstances, he having been the owner of a number of slaves and considerable real estate. The mother was born in 1787, and died November 18, 1847, both she and her husband having been consistent members of the Baptist Church. Five of their ten children are living at the present time.[2]

The history also notes that Lucy Dodson was a relative of Jefferson Davis. Presumably this was Jefferson Davis of the Confederacy, but the relationship may have been a distant cousinship, because the Davis genealogy does not show Lucy as close kin.[3] However, any relationship at all would account for the Dodson family's Southern sympathies and its strong belief in slavery.

Long after most of the Dodsons had died, a history of Camden County, Missouri, was recorded in the local newspaper, The *Reveille*. Written in 1896 it notes: "Among the first immigrants was James Dodson, who settled near the subsequent site at Glaize City. His son, Dr. J. N. B. Dodson, was one of the founders of Linn Creek and also of Glaize City. Another son, Dr. William Dodson, was a noted physician and clergyman, and Benjamin D. Dodson, a third son, was one of the county's most successful business men and best citizens. A daughter, Mrs. Lucy A. Estes, still lives near the old home. She remembers many incidents of early pioneer life, and tells of having seen three elk near her father's house the year of their arrival."[4] Not mentioned are the other six of the ten children of James and Lucy Dodson, including Mary Watt Dodson Donoho, but by 1896, Mary and most of the others were dead and probably unknown in Camden County.

Another local history reports that no definite record or tradition of the first settlers or "squatters" to make their homes in the region seems to have been preserved. The earliest settlers probably pitched their camp in 1827 on the Dry Auglaize, near what is now Chauncey, eight miles east of Linn Creek, and not far from the encampment of three tribes of Indians, among whom was a band of the Osages. "Negotiations were entered upon, and they soon exchanged sundry blankets, bridles, etc., for the possession of sufficient land for their needs. Returning to Kentucky for their families, they settled there in 1828 . . . . To the west of them lay an unbroken wilderness."[5]

Of that wilderness in Camden County, originally ninety-seven per cent was dense forest, comprising 692 square miles located in southcentral Missouri. Its main tributaries to the Osage River were the Niangua, Little Niangua and Grand Auglaize Rivers.[6] Auglaize Township got its name from the French word "glaise" meaning potter's clay. Described as "a white tenacious clay, probably fit for Potter's ware," it also had saline properties and was used as a salt lick in many areas.[7]

This was the country where Mary Donoho's family settled. "Glaize City, once a thriving community," writes historian Fern Moreland in 1983, "on the Wet Glaize Stream, is now identified mainly by a cemetery. Dr. Jim Dodson, one of the counties [sic] earliest settlers, is credited with the birth of the town. Glaize City once contained a general store, lumber mill, post office, brick kiln, and two blacksmith shops. One outstanding feature of the town was its three-story academy, where many leading citizens of the area received their education. According to legend, the academy lost its usefulness when an extra heavy snow accumulation resulted in the roof's collapsing."[8] Another account disagrees: "With the aid of the Doctors Dodson, neighbors and friends, they established the Glaize City Academy . . . . It was an impressive three-story building made of brick and slave labor . . . . The problem of teachers faced them, and since the Dodsons . . . were college graduates, they all at times worked in that capacity . . . . The building was later bought by the Iberian Academy and disman-tled and moved."[9] The town of Glaize City began its slow decline after the Civil War. It was then that the railroad extended its line, and the towns of Richland and Stoutland were built close by.[10]

More than likely, the first shelter built by the Dodson family was a log cabin. No doubt it would have been similar to one described in the Camden County history: "The Pioneer's Cabin . . . was always made of logs, sometimes hewed on two sides and sometimes not hewed at all. When hewed, the logs were put up with the flat surfaces on the inside and outside of the building. The cracks were filled with 'chinking,' and this was daubed over with mud. The form of the cabin was always an oblong square, with a huge fire-place in one end. The fireplace was set back in a crib composed of logs, with the face even with the inner wall. This crib was heavily lined with stone and mortar, built up on a hearth made of flat stones. On the top of the stone and mortar lining was made a stick and mud chimney, the latter always being entirely on the outside of the building, and extending a little above the comb of the roof. The cabin was only one story in height . . . . One or two small openings were cut out for windows.''[11]

Mary Donoho was probably born in such a log cabin in Tennessee. Her parents were married in 1804 and she was born in 1807, so she could have been the first, second or third of their ten children. Only six, or possibly seven, are accounted for and birth years are known for only four: Mary, 1807; William M. Dodson, 1811; Lucy Dodson Estes, 1816; Benjamin D. Dodson, 1827.[12] Besides James N. B. Dodson and Zilpha Dodson Brockman, a seventh child of Lucy and James may have been Penelope Dodson, born in 1818, who married B. B. Harrison and died in 1853.

Of the Dodson children who stayed in Missouri, the most prominent was Mary's brother, Dr. William M. Dodson. Like his father, he was called an ''eminent physician,'' and his medical training was standard for the time. He studied under his father and took a course of lectures at Lexington, Kentucky, in the winter of 1836-37. He also studied under his brother, Dr. James N. B. Dodson. He commenced his medical practice at Glaize City in 1838 and was the only physician in the county for many years. He had a very successful practice which extended over a circuit of forty-five miles.[13]

William Dodson's career as a Methodist minister embroiled him in a controversy following the Civil War, which had repercussions beyond Camden County. The *Jefferson City People's Tribune* blasted Dodson in an 1868 story titled ''More Pious Rascality,'': ''Dr. Wm. Dodson in 1846 sold to the Methodist Church South about two acres of ground in Camden County on the Glaze, for a church site. The Southern Methodists built a church thereon and continued its occupancy until about 1861. Dodson, an earnest Southern Methodist, went South and remained in the Confederacy until its downfall, when he returned to Missouri. In the meantime the Abolition or Northern Methodists had, without leave, taken charge of this church property. Dodson, to propitiate the irate gods of the Northern Methodist Church, unites with their church and actually sells this church property to his last love. He had no more authority to sell this property than he had to sell the property of any individual. He had given a warranty deed to the Methodist Church South . . . . Is this religion? The stealing of churches . . . has become the favorite amusement of this political church . . . . The same thing occurred at Independence and other places . . . . They ought to be ashamed of themselves. It is time this religious rascality was at an end.''[14]

Evidently Dodson wrote a fast and strong rebuttal because the *Tribune* quickly backed down and apologized: ''Dr. Wm. M. Dodson . . . writes to us from the Wet Glaze Post Office, Camden County, that the main facts contained in an article in the *Tribune* . . . are not entirely true. We are gratified to learn that the Doctor, though now a Northern Methodist, does not desire to rob the Southern Methodists of their property. Our informant may have been mistaken about this matter . . . . We would not wantonly do the Dr. a wrong or impute to him any misconduct if we knew it.''[15] In his 1892 autobiography, written the year before his death, Dodson explained the controversy: ''I owned the land at Wet Glaize Campground and was in favor of a reunion of both branches of the church . . . this they were not willing to do.''[16]

A document filed at the courthouse in Columbia in 1833 may indicate that Mary's minister brother William personally did not accept slavery. It recorded that William M. Dodson of Crawford County, Missouri, was relinquishing all his ''right title and interest in three Negro slaves, to wit: Emily, a Negro woman; Milcey Ann and Maria, Negro children, now in the possession of Augustus Hart, Constable of Columbia Township, Boone County, Missouri . . . . So relinquished is the interest I would have had as one of the heirs and distributees of James Dodson, deceased . . . .''[17] When she returned from Santa Fe in 1837, Mary would receive and accept her inheritance of three slaves from her father's estate.

A tribute to William M. Dodson's place in history appears in an article on the old Campground Church, to which he had donated the land in 1866. It reads: ''As a minister, he married them; as a physician, he treated them in their last sickness; and again, in the capacity of minister of the Gospel, he preached their funeral.

It is generally believed that he rode more miles on horseback, married more couples, and preached more funerals during his more than eighty-two years than anyone who ever lived in this part of Missouri."[18] William Dodson died 23 April 1893; the death of his wife Mildred Elvira followed three years later.

Lucy Dodson Estes, Mary Donoho's younger sister, lived forty-seven years past her husband's death and then outlived every family member of her own generation and all but two of her children. When she died at age ninety in 1906, she was known to everyone as "Aunt Lucy." *The Reveille* reported: "Mrs. Lucy Estes of Zaring, who died last Sunday at a very advanced age, was known either personally or by reputation to nearly all the people of Camden County . . . . She has lived here for nearly 75 years and was noted for great vigor, energy and strength of character. The Dodson family of which she was a member were among the earliest pioneers and most highly respected residents."[19]

The youngest of the Dodson children, Benjamin D., married Johanna Sprout, who as a child had made the copy of Sarah Horn's book about her captivity as a writing exercise. Benjamin started as a farmer but later became a successful merchant in Richland.

According to Mary's 1880 obituary, her parents moved from Tennessee to Missouri on 7 November 1831.[20] This is undoubtedly an error made by the newspaper editor fifty years later. If they were among the earliest settlers of Camden County, more than likely the Dodson family arrived in 1827. The county courthouse burned in 1902, so property records are not available on early pioneers. How long Mary lived with her parents in Glaize City is unknown, but by 1831, she was in Columbia, where she and William Donoho were married on November 27. The Boone County marriage record of that date is stated tersely and without punctuation: "I a Teacher of christianity performed the rites of marriage between Wm Donoho and Mary Dodson on the 27th of Nov 1831 being of lawful age & her parents having given their consent as witness my hand this 28th Nov 1831 — M P Wills ECC."[21]

William Donoho arrived in Boone County at least two years earlier and had bought property before their marriage. Although the relationships are circumstantial, Boone County deed records indicate several other Donohos were in Columbia at the same time and may have been related to William. It is possible that Jesse Donoho was his brother. Jesse and his wife Polly died about a year apart in 1836 and 1837. The inn or hotel business may have been a Donoho family specialty because Polly's probate records contain an invoice showing a boarder named James Haskins who paid her $31, which included his board and lodging for four weeks at $2.50 per week, plus the feeding of three yoke of oxen for two weeks at $5.25 per week.[22] Jesse and Polly left eight young children. The estate was administered by a Samuel Denham for several years and his annual reports list the children, the youngest of whom was a boy named Sidney.[23] He may have been the same Sidney Donoho who later lived in Clarksville, Texas, with his cousin, James Donoho. Sidney willed his estate of nearly $2000 to James when he died in 1904.[24] He could have been the son of Jesse Donoho because his tombstone gives his birth year as 1835, the year before Jesse died.

Connections with other Donohos in Columbia while William was there are tenuous. They include a Robert Donoho and his wife Elizabeth and an older woman named Sarah Donoho, who deeded her land to her son John in return for his promise to care for her until her death.[25]

William and Mary may have started planning the financing of their Santa Fe trip as early as 1832, when they began selling off the property William had bought before their marriage. His first purchase was in 1829 and included twelve town lots, three blocks from the town square.[26] He paid the sum of $100 for them and received a total of $275 when he later sold them in blocks of three and six. The last three were sold in January 1833, just six months before their departure for New Mexico.[27] He had also bought and sold part of a section of land, about fifty-four acres, in Boone County and made a small profit on it. According to the deed records, William disposed of all their property in Boone County before they left. However, a year and a half later, his name appeared in a delinquent tax list in the *Missouri Intelligencer.* Apparently the newspaper was zealously doing its duty in protecting the taxpayers when it accused those on the list of being "insolvent or absconded." It listed William Donoho as owing $64 for city, county and bridge taxes.[28]

Headstones of James Dodson (1772-1832) and Lucy Dodson (1787-1847) in the Glaize City Cemetery near Camdenton, Missouri. They were the father and mother of Mary Donoho. Photo by the author.

By 1831 the town of Columbia was well established. Many of the homes were still log cabins, but the first brick building was erected in 1821,[29] and many fine brick homes had been built by the mid-1820s. There is no way of knowing whether Mary and William built a house on either the fifty-four acres they owned or on one of their twelve town lots.

Their first child, Mary Ann, was born 20 October 1832. Mary's father died suddenly four days after Christmas of that same year. James Dodson's burial was one of the earliest in the Glaize City Cemetery. The old graveyard still stands in Camden County, five miles from the Pulaski County line. In the corners of four Sections: 5, 6, 31 and 32, it is located in bottomland not far from the Glaize River. Enclosed by a sturdy wire fence, the cemetery is now bounded by cornfields on two sides and is virtually impossible to find without a map and explicit directions.[30]

Only a few other families share the Glaize City Cemetery with the Dodson and Estes families. Occasionally descendants come to tend the graves and to cut the overgrowth of weeds. A tenacious black mold has covered several Dodson stones and has been scraped off in places in order to read the names. The tall thin stones of James and Lucy Dodson are worn and lichen-covered, which is understandable, since his is over one hundred fifty years old. Nearby are buried son William Dodson and his wife Mildred, daughter Lucy Estes and her husband John, and daughter Penelope. About twenty grandchildren also share the ancient little graveyard. Fifth, sixth and seventh generation progeny of the Dodsons still live in Camden and Pulaski Counties, including the names of Armstrong, Gibson, Foster, Hamlin, Snead, Puckett and Traw.

When Mary Dodson Donoho left for Santa Fe in 1833, however, her father was the only Dodson buried in the Glaize City Cemetery. Her decision to accompany her husband of sixteen months and journey almost a thousand miles from Boone County to the frontier in New Mexico when, presumably, no other woman was doing so seems to have been an extremely courageous one. But, as her son James would say of her after her death, his mother was a woman of "energy and commanding spirit."

Women on the Santa Fe Trail

*It may appear, perhaps, a little extraordinary that females should
have ventured across the Prairies under such forlorn auspices.*
—Josiah Gregg, *Commerce of the Prairies, 1844*

With her forty-five-year-old husband Samuel, nineteen-year-old Susan Shelby Magoffin arrived in Santa Fe on 31 August 1846, two weeks after General Stephen Watts Kearny's occupation of the town. She proclaimed, ''I have entered the city in a year that will always be remembered by my countrymen; and under the 'Star Spangled banner' too, the first American lady, who has come under such auspices, and some of our company seem disposed to make me the first under any circumstances that ever crossed the Plains.''[1]

The nineteen-year-old Magoffin, who spent thirty-two days in Santa Fe, then traveled on and did not return and whose splendid journal was not published for eighty years, may be forgiven her exuberant claims. What is more perplexing is why Josiah Gregg, who made nine expeditions over the Santa Fe Trail between 1831 and 1840, does not mention the American woman living in Santa Fe between 1833 and 1837, helping her husband manage a hotel, and possibly even running it herself while he was off trading.

As a single man, it seems likely that Gregg would have been one of the first to patronize a facility with an American landlady. There are two possible answers: Mary Donoho was the only American woman in Santa Fe and he did not know she was there, or there were others in addition to her and it was not considered unusual enough to mention. The second answer seems most unlikely, yet it must be considered.

Gregg wrote of other women who preceded Donoho: "It may appear, perhaps, a little extraordinary that females should have ventured across the Prairies under such forlorn auspices." The first of "the softer sex," as he called them, to travel the Santa Fe Trail were six women who had been exiled from Mexico with their husbands and traveled from west to east. On his first trip to Santa Fe in 1831, Gregg wrote: "Those who accompanied us . . . were members of a Spanish family who had been banished in 1829 in pursuance of a decree of the Mexican congress and were now returning to their homes in consequence of a suspension of the decree. Other females, however, have crossed the prairies to Santa Fe at different times, among whom I have known two respectable French ladies, who now reside in Chihuahua."[2]

The well-to-do Spanish refugees had left Santa Fe on 1 September 1829 with the Missouri-bound caravan. Their party of ten men and six women was accompanied by Colonel Jose Antonio Viscarra and a force of two hundred men (seventy-five Mexicans, ninety-one "hired whites," and thirty-four "hired Indians"), who provided escort all the way to the Arkansas. There were ninety-six traders, fewer than thirty wagons, and about two thousand head of horses, mules and jacks.[3] Many years later one of the Missouri traders gave a different account: "When we started on our homeward journey, seven priests and a number of wealthy families, comfortably fixed in wagons more like our railway coaches than ordinary wagons, accompanied us."[4] That there were comfortable vehicles, similar to railway coaches of later years, to travel in as early as 1829 is an intriguing concept. Much later on the Santa Fe Trail, large enclosed wagons called "ambulances" were used for ease in traveling, but little has been found about them in earlier trail accounts.

Another woman who may have traveled back and forth on the trail before Mary Donoho was Santa Fean Carmel Robidou. Antoine Robidou reportedly married Carmel Benevides at Santa Fe in 1828, and she accompanied him on many trips from there to Missouri. Robidou was a brother of Joseph Robidou, founder of St. Joseph, Missouri, and of prominent fur traders Francois and Louis Robidou.[5] It has since been determined that Carmel and Antoine were not married, but were among the many American traders and local women who cohabitated in New Mexico.[6]

It appears that these nine — the six Spanish exiles, two ''French ladies,'' and Carmel Robidou — were the first women to travel the Santa Fe Trail. Mary Donoho was the next, and apparently she has the distinction of being the first Anglo-American to do so.

In the early spring of 1833, Mary and William Donoho would have had to travel over a hundred miles from Columbia, Missouri, to join the spring caravan in Independence. Unusually heavy rains and muddy roads that year caused delays for everyone. The rendezvous with the military escort, scheduled for May 15 at Round Prairie, near the Missouri line, was shifted to Council Grove, over one hundred miles west.[7]

The escort, under the command of Captain William N. Wickliffe, consisted of one hundred forty-four officers and men, five supply wagons, one piece of field artillery and its accompanying ammunition wagon. The force included Captain Matthew Duncan's company of Rangers. The escort troops had been given two weeks of training for the mission by Major Bennet Riley, who had led the 1829 escort. Wickliffe's men did not reach Council Grove until June 13, the rainy weather limiting their daily marches.[8]

The *Missouri Intelligencer* reported a new location for the company on 20 July 1833:

> Letters from some of our traders as late as the 20th of June have been received in St. Louis. They were assembled at the Diamond Grove about 160 miles from Independence in this state. On the 19th an election for officers was held. Mr. C. [Charles] Bent was elected to the Captaincy; Messrs. Legrave, Barnes, Smith and Branch, Lieuts. There were 184 men belonging to the expedition, and 93 wagons, carriages, and dearborns attached to it — 63 of which were loaded with goods. The company had suffered very much from the

badness of the roads, caused by the great rains which had fallen there as everywhere else. We have understood, though the letter we have seen does not allude to it, that the traders are under the escort of a company of Rangers.[9]

Another source reports that the trading caravan was larger and totaled 103 wagons and carriages. The value of the goods was listed variously at $100,000 and $180,000, with Charles Bent's merchandise alone valued at $40,000.[10]

At the Great Bend of the Arkansas, Captain Wickliffe's men took the more direct "dry route" where they lost the trail and their horses suffered from lack of water and grazing. After rejoining the caravan, the escort accompanied it as far as the Lower Crossing of the Arkansas. They parted company there on July 11, the soldiers returning to Fort Leavenworth, where they arrived on August 4,[11] also the date of Wickliffe's "Report of his Santa Fe Expedition," written to Major Riley. He commended Lieutenants Freeman and Hoffman for discharging their duties correctly and efficiently and noted, "We owe much to the industry and skill of Doct. L. Perry who was engaged to accompany the escort as Physician & Surgeon, his professional duties were rendered with cheerfulness at all times, and in the opinion of all with great skill, and we know with entire success."[12]

The traders, accompanied by Captain Richard B. Lee, who had been with the escort and was on leave from the army, made their way through Mexican territory and reached Santa Fe on August 4.[13] It seems inconceivable that of the 328 persons in the caravan, not one left a written record that a woman and baby were in the wagon train on their way to Santa Fe.

How Mary and her nine-month-old daughter, Mary Ann, fared under the summer sun on the Kansas prairie is a matter for conjecture. Mary and William may well have had both Conestoga wagons and a carriage on the trip. Of the 93 or 103 vehicles in the expedition, depending on which report was correct, only 63 were loaded with goods.[14] This left the remaining thirty or forty for passengers. An account of a later caravan includes a description: "The plain was covered with the long files of their whitetopped wagons, [and] the close black carriages in which the traders travel and sleep.''[15] This suggests that the carriages were the preferred vehicle in which to ride. Mary Ann would still have been in the nursing stage and certainly it would have given mother and baby more privacy.

It is possible that William and Mary took along a servant from Missouri. Her father owned slaves and although she would not inherit some of his until after she returned to Missouri, no doubt she was accustomed to having domestic help. If they had a hired helper along on the journey, the backbreaking work of the trail — cooking over an open fire or gathering fuel — would have been eased considerably.

Mary's actual experiences can only be speculated upon, but we can look at another woman's journey to learn of the daily routine, the clothing and other ways of the trail, as well as the joys and perils. That woman is Marian Sloan Russell, whose colorful memoirs bring the trail to life. She first traveled the trail fifteen years after Mary Donoho, but very little had changed. The caravans still lumbered slowly across the prairie as they had with the Donohos. Even though the story was written late in her life, the affection and excitement Marian felt for the trail was as clear as it had been when she was a young girl, eighty-five years earlier.

The year was 1852. Marian recalled the first of her five trips:

> The dread cholera was raging in Fort Leavenworth the day
> our white-hooded wagons set sail on the western prairies.
> Our little city of tents dissolved like snow in a summer sun.
> Captain Aubry broke camp first; his great wagon swayed out
> onto the trail . . . his powerful voice calling orders to follow.[16]
> Minute impressions flash before me; the sun-bonnetted
> women, the woolen trousered men, little mother in flounced
> gingham, brother Will walking in long strides by our driver.
> Each morning . . . men began rolling out from under the
> wagons. There stretched out before us was a new-coined
> day . . . under a glorious turquoise sky. Packing was done
> swiftly and the mules hitched to the wagons. Drivers were
> calling, ''Get up there! Come along, Boys!'' Bull whips were
> cracking and all about the heavy wagons began groaning.
> The mules leaned into the collar and the great wheels began
> a steady creaking . . . .[17]

For the color and feeling of the Santa Fe Trail, Marian Russell's moving story cannot be matched, and no doubt Mary Donoho's experience of forty-six days and nights on the trail was similar.

The three Texas women rescued by William Donoho, whose experiences are discussed in chapter six, are the next three Anglo-American women who traveled the Santa Fe Trail. Rachael Plummer and Mrs. Harris, the second and third, had reached Santa Fe by tortuous Indian trails, but they returned to Missouri by way of the Santa Fe Trail. They were with the Donohos in the wagon train which left Santa Fe in haste following the uprising against Governor Albino Perez in August 1837. A year later they were followed by a fourth, Sarah Horn, another captive who returned to Missouri over the trail with the Workman-Rowland caravan, under instructions from William Donoho.

According to James Donoho's 1887 letter to John Henry Brown, another U. S. woman was in Santa Fe in 1838 and gave birth to a child: "While in Santa Fe it was settled to my satisfaction, that my second sister-born in 1835, and myself, born in 1837, were the first white Americans born in Santa Fe, New Mexico. The honor or distinction (if it can so be called) had been claimed by others in behalf of one born there in 1838, but which was later than my own and sister's."[18] This unknown mother was the fifth Anglo-American woman to travel the trail.

These five women — Mary Donoho, Rachael Plummer, Mrs. Harris, Sarah Horn and the unnamed mother — must now take their places in history as the first Anglo-American women to travel the Santa Fe Trail. Susan Shelby Magoffin, who arrived in 1846, has long been celebrated as the first. History must now record that she was at least the sixth.

It is possible that the discovery of these five may only be the beginning. There were two other women who made the journey after they did and before Susan Magoffin in 1846. In 1841 a "nice little Dutch woman, accompanying her husband," traveled the trail three years after the Donohos left. She came with the spring caravan which totaled eighty-seven males and one female. Also in her caravan were others "going . . . for pleasure, some for health, and . . . for the curiosities and botanical plants.'' In the party was naturalist William Gambel.[19]

In March 1846, before Susan Magoffin arrived in August, Soledad Abreu Leitensdorfer made the journey East with her husband's caravan.[20] With that total of eight women, plus the nine before Mary Donoho, seventeen all told, it seems illogical to presume that not one other women came in the nine years between Mary Donoho's departure and Susan Magoffin's arrival. Their names may yet come to light.

One fact is certain. By the late 1840s women had begun the trek down the Santa Fe Trail in earnest. On 21 May 1848, the *Santa Fe Republican* reported: ''We understand that there are several American families on the road to this place. This is what we like to see and the time is not far distant where we shall see this country thickly settled by industrious and enterprising Americans.''[21] And come they did, men and women. When the first United States census was taken in 1850, there were over thirty women from the United States living in Santa Fe.[22] With each successive census the count of Anglo-American-born women increased.

The two oldest tombstones marking women's graves in Santa Fe cemeteries bear mute witness to the move's hardships. Kate Kingsbury, wife of merchant John L. Kingsbury, died at the Lower Crossing of the Arkansas in 1857. A consumptive, she was on her second trip to Santa Fe. Her husband was prepared with a coffin in his stores of merchandise and her body was brought on to Santa Fe.[23] Catharine Gorman, wife of Baptist missionary Samuel Gorman, went with him to Laguna Pueblo in 1852, lived there seven years, bore two babies and sometimes did not see another Anglo-American woman for a year at a time. Her health broken, she died in Santa Fe in 1862.[24]

Among the thirty United States women in the 1850 territorial census are wives of traders, merchants, government officials, and more missionaries. By the 1860 census, the number of Anglo women in Santa Fe rose to nearly fifty and included ten nuns at Loretto Academy. None of the names are the same as on the previous census. Unquestionably, there were many other women who came and went on the trail in the ten years between each census. If those numbers were known the total would be much higher. The 1870 federal count reported that just over sixty Anglo women made Santa Fe their home. That number would increase dramatically when the railroad arrived in February 1880 and marked the end of the Santa Fe Trail. When the census was taken in June of that year, over two hundred Anglo-American women were living in Santa Fe.[25] Most of them would stay longer than the first pioneer of their number, Mary Donoho.

The Santa Fe of the Donohos

*My parents liked Santa Fe, and doubtless my father would have
spent his life there had it not been for the dangers threatening his
family from the turbulent spirit of Mexicans and Indians.*
—James B. Donoho, 1887 Letter

*T*here is virtually no extant record of Mary and William
Donoho's residence in Santa Fe between 1833 and 1837.
No guia, or passport of the time survives, no known
manifest of trading goods bears their name; and no mention of
them occurs in records of *estranjeros*, or foreigners, in New Mexico.[1] To date only one document has been found in New Mexico
primary source records which shows a Donoho was ever there. After
the family left in 1837 and William returned in 1838 to put their
affairs in order, he witnessed the transfer of a mule to another
American trader.[2] For now, then, peripheral knowledge must suf-
fice, the picture of Santa Fe formed by a few individuals, not one
of whom mentions the Donoho name, who lived there or wrote
about the Donoho years.

When the caravan of Mary and William Donoho approached
Santa Fe in August 1833, they undoubtedly experienced mixed
emotions. There was probably relief at having arrived safely; curiosity, and perhaps some apprehension about the life ahead of them.
But assuredly there was exuberance. Author R. L. Duffus called
it "the greatest moment of life upon the Trail . . . for Santa Fe had

always the lure of strangeness and adventure. It was not a peaceful coming home, it was an excitement which set men's hearts thumping, made them throw their hats in the air, made them stand up in their stirrups, and yell like wild Indians and shoot off their firearms."[3]

Arriving in Santa Fe in late summer, when Missouri would have been at its hot and humid worst, the Donohos may have been delightfully surprised at the high dry climate. Josiah Gregg was taken with the climate. "A sultry day," he wrote, "from Santa Fe north, is of very rare occurrence. The summer nights are usually so cool and pleasant that a pair of blankets constitutes an article of comfort seldom dispensed with."[4]

Upon seeing Santa Fe for the first time, writers have given many diverse descriptions of its appearance, ranging from a town of "brick-kilns" to one with walls of "dazzling whiteness." Ralph Twitchell affectionately describes how the traders saw it as they ascended the crest of the lower spur of the Sangre De Cristos and looked down upon the town: "New Mexico's ancient capital, the Mecca of the Missourian, came into view, nestling in a beautiful valley, with here and there occasional groups of trees, and skirted with corn and wheat fields, the flat roofed houses with their newly whitewashed walls afforded a most pleasing prospect."[5]

Duffus' description of Santa Fe is humorous but perceptive:

> At first sight the town was not much to look at. It was possible to be utterly disgusted with it at first sight, second sight, and last sight. To enjoy it thoroughly one had to have a flair for such things. Literal-minded persons did not, puritanical persons did not. But there were those who longed for it as a sailor longs for the sea. For some men, perhaps, it was an antidote for the smugness, hypocrisy and over-fastidiousness they hated in the American civilization of their day. But for all who came it was at least rest and food and the end of peril. The joy of the seasoned plainsmen, with forty days of uninhabited wilderness behind them, could not have been much greater if this indeed had been Cibola, the shining city, or Quivera, in which everyone ate from dishes of gold and the women fastened their hair with diamonds.[6]

Santa Fe in 1847. This engraving shows Santa Fe as it looked to travelers as they came over the last hill above the city on Old Santa Fe Trail. Except for Fort Marcy on the hill overlooking the town, it would have been little changed since the time of the Donohos. Courtesy Museum of New Mexico, negative number 21149.

Josiah Gregg agreed that an arrival in Santa Fe was something special and he waxed eloquent: "Even the animals seemed to participate in the humor of their riders, who grew more and more merry and obstreperous as they descended towards the city. I doubt, in short, whether the first sight of the walls of Jerusalem was beheld by the crusaders with much more tumultuous and soul-enrapturing joy." But he was not so complimentary about the physical appearance of the town on his first visit, writing: "Oh, we are approaching the suburbs!" He saw the cornfields and what he supposed to be brick-kilns scattered in every direction and commented upon it. A friend at his elbow said, "It is true those are heaps of unburnt bricks, nevertheless they are houses — this is the city of Santa Fe."[7]

A colorful description of the town scene is given by Francisco Perea in his memoirs. He and his family came from Bernalillo to Santa Fe shortly after the rebellion against Governor Albino Perez. The Pereas of the town of Bernalillo were a prestigious family of the "lower country," and were instrumental in pressing Manuel Armijo into service following the rebellion. It led to Armijo becoming governor. Perea was only a boy when he came to Santa Fe and the memoirs were written seventy-five years later, about 1912. His writings shed some light on the activities and appearance of the town during the winter of 1837-1838.

The Perea family arrived about the time the Donohos left. He remembers, "Upon our arrival at the capital we found the place full of soldiers, citizens, and a miscellaneous gathering of humanity of all stations of life, the plaza being crowded with all kinds of vehicles, beginning with the cart [carreta] that was made entirely of wood . . . to the well-constructed wagon that had brought a consignment of merchandise over the Santa Fe Trail; together with teamsters, camp-cooks, roustabouts, horses, mules, burros, pigs, and goats. Some were about their camp-fires preparing their food, while others were feeding and caring for their animals."[8]

Whether Mary and William found the exterior appearance of Santa Fe appalling or inviting will never be known, but the interiors of the thick, well-insulated buildings may have been a pleasant surprise to them. As Matthew Field reported in 1840:

The interior of one of these mud built houses, particularly
when arranged with the assistance of American taste forms a
very comfortable and by no means inelegant dwelling . . . .
In some of the better houses you will find an apartment set
apart as a parlor, this invariably being also the sleeping
room; during the day the beds are folded close up to the
walls, and covered with the handsome (sometimes really
beautiful) Spanish blankets, forming a succession of sofas all
around the room . . . . These blankets are the chief sign of
wealth among the people, and their elegance and number
forms the pride of every housekeeper; the best of them are
so closely woven that they can be used for holding water,
and the bright colors that never fade are mingled through
them generally with very tasteful and ingenious disposition.⁹

Santa Fe buildings were considered very practical. Perea describes
the architecture thus: ''Every class of building, being constructed
of adobe bricks and flat-roofed, precluded any great effort at archi-
tectural finish, and about all that was attempted in that way was
in the finishing of doors, windows and some ornamental work about
the heads of columns and posts of porches. The glazing of windows had not been introduced at that time, window glass being
almost entirely unknown.''¹⁰

Perea gives the closest physical description of the Plaza during
the time of the Donohos. Writing of Santa Fe after they left in 1837,
he is not complimentary:

Near the northeast corner of the plaza, which was then
surrounded on its four sides by flat-roofed one-story
buildings, with portals (porches) in front of them, were
three cottonwood trees of the mountain variety, and opposite the Palace (the capitol) stood a flagstaff, from the top
of which was displayed the Mexican flag in all its glory; and
the four entrances at the corners of the square were guarded,
each with a single cannon of small caliber.

The square was then a dirty, unsightly place almost to a
degree unbelievable. In fact the public square, which is now
a scene of beauty and one of the most noted places of its
kind in our whole country, was in the years 1837 and 1838,
totally destitute of any other ornament than I have mentioned

. . . and the people seemed to be satisfied with these conditions. Opposite the Palace stood the military church, called La Castrense, then the handsomest building of its kind in the capital city . . . Don Manuel Chaves, father of Amado Chaves, Esq., built and owned the finest dwelling house in Santa Fe. This structure was built four-square, enclosing a court, and was finished with portals all around outside, and also on the insides bordering the court . . . . There were no gable roofs in the entire capital at that time and the residences were scattered over a large area, with more or less ground enclosed with adobe walls, in which were gardens, orchards, corrals and stables.[11]

Although Mary Donoho had no wood floor (only one building in Santa Fe, the mercantile store of John Skolly, boasted a plank floor), her smooth adobe floors were undoubtedly firm and satisfactory as long as they did not get wet. Because of operating a hotel, she may also have had an additional luxury — a covering for the floors. Said one writer, "Occasionally a coarse domestic fabric called *xerga* was spread upon the floor, the ceilings were commonly of uncovered beams, though muslin was sometimes tacked across them; or the interstices were filled in with small sticks, or *latias* . . . . The furniture was as simple as furniture could well be, and still merit the name . . . . Cooking was done in earthen vessels and bread was baked in outdoor ovens. Mattresses covered with blankets served as seats as well as couches. Utensils of iron were very rare."[12] If Mary and William Donoho left Missouri with the intention of opening a hotel in Santa Fe, more than likely they would have brought with them items such as metal pots and cooking utensils, which would have been essential in their daily operations.

In their first impressions of Santa Fe, early writers were never impartial. They either loved it or hated it. The puritanical Rufus Sage declared, "There are no people on the continent of America, whether civilized or uncivilized . . . more miserable in condition or despicable in morals than the mongrel race inhabiting New Mexico."[13] Even though Susan Magoffin was also quite puritan in her ways, she was more charitable in her impressions of the native New Mexicans. "What an inquisitive, quick people they are!" she exclaimed. And later, "What a polite people these Mexicans are . . . .

This morning I have rather taken a little protege, a little market girl . . . she came in and we had a long conversation . . . . Just to see the true politeness and ease displayed by that child is truly [amazing], 'twould put many a mother in the U. S. to the blush.''[14]

A well known woman citizen of the town during the Donoho's stay in Santa Fe is wonderfully described by Duffus, but he too perpetuates the stories of Gregg, Magoffin and Twitchell when he writes:

> Senora Dona Gertrudes Barcelo, a successful woman whose manners ran counter to the strict Puritan standards of the early Anglo newcomers to Santa Fe, came down from Taos, her lovely eyes flaming with ambition, got a place in a gambling house, made some lucky bets on the side, purchased a gambling business of her own, and became a prominent figure in the city's social life. Beautiful in her youth, she wore false teeth and a wig in her old age, but maintained to the last very much of an air. The elite of Santa Fe thronged her elegantly fitted monte rooms. She was, everyone admiringly conceded, the most skillful monte card dealer in the whole world.[15]

Actually, Tules was probably born in Mexico and came to Tome in Valencia County by 1823, where her parents were referred to as Don and Dona Barcelo by the Padre of Tome. This was a title bestowed only on families of high rank and contradicts the myth that she was of low birth. Tules married in Tome and she and her husband moved to Santa Fe, where eventually she did open a fine gambling house. But according to Fray Angelico Chavez, the scandals circulated about her running a brothel and being the mistress of Governor Manuel Armijo are totally undocumented and simply fabricated and perpetuated by early writers.[16]

Perhaps the truth lies somewhere in between. Nevertheless, Dona Tules may have been a welcome guest in the Donoho's hotel. It is doubtful that William and Mary were particularly prudish because many years later in Clarksville, Texas, Mary served liquors in her tavern and gave balls at the Donoho House.

Mary Donoho may well have been acquainted with Dona Tules, since the two were not much different in age and apparently shared one trait in common: red hair. When Tules was married in 1823, she was twenty-three years of age, making her but seven years Donoho's senior.[17] In her fictionalized biography of Tules, *The Wind Leaves No Shadow*, Ruth Laughlin claims that the Santa Fean was red-haired. Laughlin may have gotten the information from Santa Fe old-timers, among whom apparently it was common knowledge.[18] According to Mary Donoho's great-great-grandson, a portrait pictured her with red hair, so Tules and Mary Donoho may have shared that feature. Since Indian captive Rachael Plummer also had red hair, during her brief stay in town, there may have been at least three redheaded women in Santa Fe of the 1830s.

If Mary Donoho was the only Anglo-American woman in Santa Fe from 1833 to 1837, she would have been unique among "two hundred foreign strangers, most Americans." Her first three years, until the rebellion against Governor Albino Perez in 1837, were probably fairly serene, the only excitement occurring whenever a trading caravan arrived at the Plaza. More than likely, Mary's time was devoted to the daily duties of the hotel and her children.

The Donoho's firstborn, Mary Ann, was ten months old when they arrived in Santa Fe in August 1833. Daughter Harriet was born fourteen months later, in January 1835. James arrived sixteen months after that, in May 1837. Unless she brought an experienced female servant from Missouri, no doubt Mary engaged a midwife from the community for the birth of the two. Probably she also learned to speak Spanish soon after settling in Santa Fe.

If, as James said, his parents liked Santa Fe, they undoubtedly made close friends there. Among them may have been some of the Anglo-Hispanic couples. Between 1829 and 1836, eight Anglo men are known to have married native New Mexican women in Santa Fe. James Conklin, a French Canadian, married Juana Ortiz in 1829. He lived not far from where the Presbyterian Church now stands and was the only American in that area to live in a "grand house." It was probably on or near the property where his son-in-law, Pinckney R. Tully, later built the house on Grant Street which still bears his name.[19]

Two Anglo-American men married Santa Fe women in 1832, one year after Mary and William were married in Missouri. The two couples were Pedro and Marcelina Coy and Juan Rafael and Maria Newman. The men had taken Spanish first names, usually the Spanish equivalent of their own, which was not uncommon.

Five other marriages took place while the Donohos were in Santa Fe. All five occurred in 1836, just a year before the Donohos left, but in a community the size of Santa Fe, the chances are great that all were acquainted with William and Mary. They were: Julian and Magdalena Gauthier, Antonio and Maria Grillette, Juan and Maria Mars, Antonio and Juana Smith and Luis and Marcelina Washington.[20]

William also made friends in Taos. Evidently he took trading goods there from time to time, because he is reported to have "returned to the ancient city of the Holy Faith and the nearby Indian village of Taos, where he went often to trade.[21] Two of his friends there were William Workman and Thomas Rowland. Before he left in 1837 to take his family, together with Rachael Plummer and Mrs. Harris, to Missouri, he arranged with the two Taos men to take charge of Sarah Horn after he paid to have her ransomed.

In 1837 when the turbulence of the rebellion against Governor Albino Perez erupted, the City of Holy Faith was a frightening place to be. Eyewitness Charles Blumner, a thirty-one year-old native of Germany, arrived in Santa Fe in 1836 and lived there for forty years, during which time he worked as a gold miner, clerk, merchant, census taker, accountant, county sheriff, U. S. Marshal and Territorial collector and treasurer. Sometime after the 1837 rebellion he wrote his mother in Germany:

> I, myself, made some money in this business, but lost it during a revolution in the year 1837 in Santa Fe in August, about $300. Which I had loaned to the leading men of the city. Part I loaned and to others I had sold on credit. The revolution was bloody. People oppressed for a long time and with bad government were stirred up and large numbers confronted Santa Fe. The governor confronted them, lost the battle and fled with other officials, was captured and was killed in a very bloody manner. The governor, Don Alvino Perez was killed and his head cut from his body; Don Santiago Abrevio [Abreu] had his tongue cut out of his throat,

he was one of the most influential and most hated, his
brothers, Don Jesus Maria Alarid, the secretary of the governor and a few others were killed. The bodies were mutilated
and brought in front of my door to the cemetary [sic]. After
a few weeks it became quiet, I went then with an American
to Chihuahua.[22]

In an 1841 letter to his sister, Blumner again wrote details about
the American traders at the time of the 1837 revolt:

We, ourselves, were strangers here, were prepared for battle [afraid] that the peons and revolutionaries would damage
the houses and shops of foreigners. At this time, we were
about 200 foreign strangers here, most Americans. Just at
the time the caravan from Missouri arrived. The shops of the
Americans here are all in a chain (row) on the street at the
marketplace. Here we were assembled, awaiting the attack.
We had at the minimum 500 to 600 loaded guns and
prepared for a hot battle. Saddled horses and mules stood
prepared in the courtyards and stables so that we could
escape if necessary. But everything went quietly.[23]

Unfortunately, no personal account gives the names of the
American ''strangers'' who organized the defense. Because he was
a permanent resident, William Donoho could well have been one
of the leaders of the group. With only two hundred men and six
hundred guns, each man must have had two or three weapons.

Governor Albino Perez was assassinated and decapitated on Agua
Fria Road southwest of Santa Fe 8 August 1837. His head was carried on a pole to the rebel camp in Santa Fe and kicked around
by the insurgents. The naked corpse could neither be clothed or
buried until August 10th.[24]

This incident prompted William Donoho to take his family back
to Missouri. They left in late August or early September because
when Sarah Horn was released from captivity about September 18,
1837, she wrote: ''I expected to meet with Mrs. Harris, but she had
left for the States with the traders, who had started earlier in the
season than usual, in consequence of the war which was raging in
Santa Fe between the Spaniards and Indians. They had killed the
governor, and the American traders were in constant alarm. Many

of them kept their gold belted round them, and their mules saddled day and night, not knowing what moment they might have to flee for their lives."[25]

After attending to matters in Missouri and Texas, Donoho hastened back to Santa Fe to look after his property and business.[26] While there, on 8 August 1838, he was called upon to sign a document supporting the statement of trader Luis Lee that a "dark-colored mule with a brand on the edge of its flanks" had been sold to Julian J. Smitte [Smith], who was given a proper bill of sale.[27] It bears his signature and is the only known document showing Donoho was ever in New Mexico. Donoho completed his business and returned to his family in Missouri, ending the Donohos' association with Santa Fe.

The Old Fonda

After disposing of a large quantity of freight which they brought in with them, Mr. Donoho engaged in the hotel business on the Plaza . . . the celebrated "old Fonda" or Exchange Hotel.
— *The Santa Fe New Mexican,* 19 August 1885

*P*opular belief maintains that a hotel has stood on the southeast corner of the Santa Fe Plaza since the town began. In his 1962 history, *La Fonda-The Inn of Santa Fe*, Peter Hertzog (the pen name of Philip St. George Cooke III) claims:

> The corner of San Francisco and Shelby Streets in Santa Fe is the oldest hotel corner in the United States. Some say the first Fonda was built there in 1609; but there are no records to that effect. It is known, however, through old Spanish documents, that a *fonda*, or inn, or tavern, had stood on that corner for hundreds of years.[1]

To date, however, no historian has found such "old Spanish documents," and author John Sherman is more guarded in his assertion: "Legend has it that a hotel has been on this site almost ever since there's been a Santa Fe. It is known, at least, that a hotel did exist here for most if not all of the nineteenth century."[2]

There is no known record establishing when the house and other buildings of the old Fonda were first used as lodging for travelers.

*Earliest photo of the old Fonda. The Exchange Hotel in 1855, eighteen
years after the Donoho's ran it. Known as the Fonda before Kearny came
in 1846, it became the U. S. Hotel, then the Exchange. Courtesy
Museum of New Mexico, negative No. 10685.*

The Urrutia map of Santa Fe in 1766 shows a series of attached
houses facing what is now San Francisco Street, from the Church
to the Plaza. Southwest of the Plaza corner, now old Santa Fe Trail,
there appears to be a wall, encompassing a large area.[3]

Whether these were the beginnings of the Fonda is uncertain,
but a clue may exist in an 1836 list of property owners of Santa Fe.
It begins with the property of the Senor Vicar and the Parish
Church, where St. Francis Cathedral stands today, on the "Calle
Principal de la Ciudad," or Main Street of the City, and ends at
the house of Dona Gertrudes Barcelo, the famed Dona Tules, in
the vicinity of the present Santa Fe County Courthouse. The list
includes all the buildings on the Plaza and the houses on the Rio
Chiquita, or Little River. A preface to the list notes which streets
and houses are included and ends: " . . . and the houses of the Rio
Chiquita, from the one known by the name of 'Los Estados Unidos'
(The United States), inclusive, as far as the Guadalupe Bridge."[4]

San Francisco Street, circa 1850. Adobe houses and shops lead toward the old Parroquia, where St. Francis Cathedral stands today. Photo Historian Dr. Richard Rudisill believes Santa Fe would have looked virtually the same in the 1830s. Courtesy U. S. Signal Corps Collection in the Museum of New Mexico, negative number 11330.

A house known as "The United States" in Santa Fe in 1836 is an astonishing piece of information. Why would it be called by that name? The most logical answer is that it was where the American traders stayed. Very possibly, it was the hotel run by William and Mary Donoho from 1833 to 1837. The year is right, and at least half of the location is correct. It would have been on what is now the south half of the La Fonda Hotel property. The north La Fonda half would have included the Plaza corner fronting on San Francisco Street and Old Santa Fe Trail. If the Rio Chiquita began then, as Water Street does now, at the east end of La Fonda, then the house known as "The United States," and owned by Don Francisco Ortiz and Don Higinio Munos, faced not only the "little river" on its south, but also the Santa Fe Trail on its west side.

It may be only a coincidence, but judging from its location on the list, the owner of the adjoining Plaza corner parcel may have been the same Don Francisco Ortiz with a different partner or relative, Don Ignacio Ortiz. The Donohos could have leased the two properties separately but used them jointly. In any case, the family was living in the old house which became the Exchange Hotel because Harriet and James Donoho were born there.

Although there are no accounts of the Donohos' hotel experience, Ralph Emerson Twitchell's romantic 1912 account of La Fonda is suggestive:

> The most notable landmark of the Santa Fe Trail was at its terminus, the adobe hotel that still stands, in part, at the southwest [southeast] corner of the plaza; from the very beginning to its close, it was the end of the great highway of commerce. This one-story structure and its great corral, with adobe walls almost as high as those of the hostelry, was the destination of the great caravans of Conestoga wagons which crossed the plains annually for more than fifty years. It was the rendezvous of the scouts, pioneers, and plainsmen from the earliest days of the trail down to the building of the great transcontinental railways, when a new era was inaugurated. Its gameing [sic] tables were the attraction that lured the prospectors, soldiers, traders, trappers, and mountaineers for miles around, and its liquid cheer soon gave to the tenderfoot sojourner all the courage, dash, and daredevil spirit of the true son of the desert. When the railway was built into Santa Fe the Fonda fell upon evil days. Its patronage began to decline with the construction of more modern accommodations and late in the last century it was abandoned for hotel purposes.[5]

In his 1925 work, *Old Santa Fe*, Ralph Emerson Twitchell quotes J. Josiah Webb's *Memoirs* in 1844: "On the southeast corner was the residence of one of the Pinos and only one or two stores or *tiendajones* till you came to the corner of the street leading to the 'Rio Chiquita' . . . ." In a footnote Twitchell adds, "This residence, during the American occupation period, or shortly after New Mexico became a Territory of the United States, was rented for hotel pur-

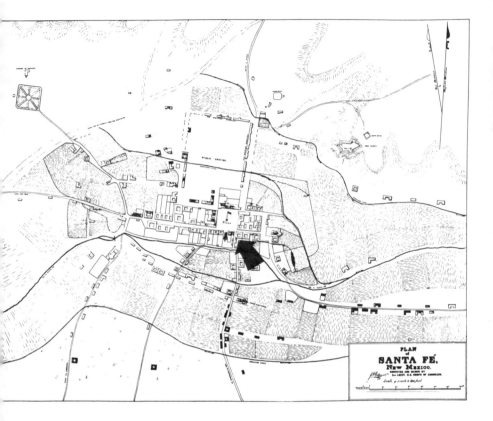

Gilmer Map of 1846. Nine years after Mary and William Donoho were in Santa Fe. The buildings housing the old Fonda are built around patios at the southeast corner of the Plaza. Arrow shows location of hotel.

poses and was known as the *Fonda*, — an inn, or tavern on the original site of the present (1925) hotel of that name.''[6]

There is no way of knowing if the Pinos owned the property which became the hotel or if they were renting it. According to the 1836 property list, the first and second properties belonged to the Senor Vicar and the Parish Church. House number three was owned by Don Juan Rafael Ortiz, probably the property where the La Fonda Carriage House now stands. If local tradition is correct, it was the house rented by Samuel and Susan Magoffin for the thirty-two days they were in Santa Fe in 1846. Susan said it was ''situated under the shadow of 'la inglesia,' (the church).''[7] The property was bought and sold several times, but Eugene A. Fiske bought it in 1881 and his family lived there until 1912.[8]

House number four was owned by Don Manuel Pino and number five by Justo Pino. This Pino house was still owned by him in the 1850s. It was the eastern boundary of the Exchange Hotel property listed in the deed records at that time. House number five, owned by Francisco and Ignacio Ortiz, is the one assumed to be the Fonda. Whether these calculations are correct is open to question, but when deeds began to be recorded in 1850, this conclusion seems the most logical one. It is also supported by a letter of 15 October 1855 from merchant William S. Messervy to his partner John M. Kingsbury. The partners claim to the hotel was being threatened by parties named Pino and Baca. According to Messervy:

> Now it appears strange — that for *five years* no question is
> raised as to the title and all the parties being in sight of the
> property and it on two different occasions exposed to public
> sale. My opinion is the original sale was a good one, and the
> claim of Pino and Baca is only a piece of Mexican Rascality
> to get possession of what they know they have no claim
> to . . . I believe the title was wholly in the old lady (Mr. Or-
> tiz's mother) and that for a sufficient consideration she sold
> to Reynolds.[9]

The first known legal description of the property does not appear in Santa Fe County deed records until 1850, twelve years after Donoho returned to Santa Fe for the last time. Since William Donoho returned to Santa Fe in 1838 ''to try to recover what they had in their haste, been compelled to leave behind in the shape of property, merchandise, mules, horses, etc.,''[10] real estate may have been involved, but if so, the transactions are lost to history. However, if Donoho had a lease on the hotel property, he could have renegotiated it on his return, and a lease would have been consistent with later transactions on the property.

The first extant document on the hotel, dated 16 April 1850 is a contract between Francisco Ortiz y Delgado (whether this is the Francisco Ortiz of 1836 is uncertain) and two American partners, Charles Rumley and William O. Ardinger. It sets up a lease for ''a certain House situated on the East side of the Plaza . . . known as the Exchange containing two rooms fronting on the Plaza, for the term of Ten Years . . . at the monthly rent of twenty five Dollars.'' In addition, Rumley and Ardinger were to ''build two new rooms above, the same size of those below and will build on a new Portal below with a Plaza above.''[11] The citing of ''two rooms fronting on the Plaza'' is not what one would expect in a description of the old Fonda, but it may have been worded in that way because the building addition was to be made only to those two rooms.

The lease with Ardinger and Rumley was short-lived. Thirteen months later they transferred it to S. C. Florence and Francisco Baca y Ortiz, but the contract was strangely changed. Dated 12 May 1851, it states: ''Upon the condition that they build a house as described in the within lease and it is not to be used as a hotel or a house for vending liquors . . . and paying all dues from the time the Exchange was Burnt (March 21th [sic] 1851).''[12] The rebuilt structure soon functioned as a hotel again, until it was torn down in 1919 to make way for the first phase of the present La Fonda.

Francisco Perea's account of 1837-38 in Santa Fe provides a good perspective on Santa Fe lodging. His description may come the closest to what the hotel was like during the four years the Donohos were in it:

> The hotels (*mesones*) were all of a very primitive kind, where travelers and others could obtain meals and lodging, and also shelter and feed for horses and other animals. The food was wholly prepared after the Mexican customs, and the favorite dish of chili, prepared in one way or another, was seldom absent from the menu. Native wine

(vino del pais) was served at the table when desired. The beds were scrupulously clean and in every way inviting for repose. Fireplaces built into the adobe walls were used for both heating and cooking purposes, there being no stoves of any sort at that time. Rates for the entertainment of transient, as well as local guests, were very reasonable, and the conventional amenities of the hostelers in the entertainment of their guests was without fault.[13]

It can perhaps be assumed that the Donohos entered into the popular local customs by having gambling and balls at the hotel for the traders and local people. Perea notes that there were a great many more dance halls *(salas de baile)* at that time than churches, of which there were five.[14] In her fictionalized account of Dona Tules' life, Ruth Laughlin portrays her heroine attending a public *baile* at La Fonda in the year 1834.[16] The Donohos might indeed have been her hosts.

Mary Donoho's four years spent helping to run the hotel in Santa Fe probably taught her the skills of organization and management. She probably oversaw a large staff of local employees. What with three children under five and overseeing the cooking and cleaning necessary for the hotel, more than likely there were few idle hours. However, experience served her well. Thirty years old when she left Santa Fe, within three years she was helping her husband manage a new hotel in Clarksville, Texas. At the age of forty, Mary Donoho would be widowed and doing it all alone. Her success there made it evident that the old Fonda in Santa Fe had been a good training ground.

Captives of the Comanches

I have no language to express my gratitude to Mrs. Donoho. I found in her a mother . . . a sister . . . a friend . . . one who was continually pouring the sweet oil of consolation into my wounded and trembling soul.
— Rachael Plummer, *The Rachael Plummer Narrative, 1838*

*I*n the year 1836 two tragic dramas were unfolding in Texas. In two separate incidents, three women — Sarah Horn, Mrs. Harris and Rachael Plummer — were captured and enslaved by the Comanche Indians. They survived and were rescued in New Mexico. Each was personally rescued by William Donoho or under his instructions, and their lives became linked with the Donohos.

The first drama occurred in March 1836, when a group of settlers from the ill-fated Dolores colony of Dr. John Charles Beales was attacked by Indians. In its two years the settlement in the southernmost part of Texas, near the town of Laredo, had not prospered. A number of families had already left and on 10 March 1836 another group abandoned the colony. General Santa Anna had invaded Texas and in order to avoid Santa Anna's troops, which were near enough for the cannon to be heard, the Dolores party had left the main road. They were making their way through wild Texas country, hoping to reach the coast by way of San Patricio, on the lower Nueces River, when they encountered a band of fifty or sixty Comanches.

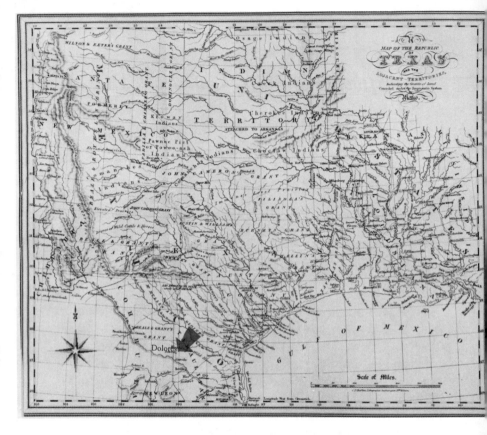

Texas map showing Beale's Grant, circa 1841. In the southern part of Texas, near the town of Dolores where Sarah Horn and Mrs. Harris were captured by the Comanches in 1836. From The Rise, Progress and Prospects of the Republic of Texas *by William Kennedy.*

The group of eleven men, two women and three children included John Horn, his wife Sarah, their two sons, John and Joseph, and a Mr. and Mrs. Harris with their baby girl. The attack occurred on the fourth of April and nine of the men, including Horn, were slain instantly. The two women and their children were abducted and the next morning the infant daughter of Mrs. Harris was killed when the Comanches repeatedly threw her to the ground. The two surviving men, one of whom was Mr. Harris, were then brought before the women and killed with arrows and lances.

It was the beginning of a long and difficult captivity for the two women. After her release, Sarah Horn wrote a story relating her experiences, eighty excruciating pages of the miseries she and her two little boys suffered. It was first published in 1839 and again in 1853. The 1839 edition, which became extremely rare, carried the ponderous title, *A Narrative of the Captivity of Mrs. Horn, and Her Two Children, with Mrs. Harris, by the Camanche Indians, After They Had Murdered Their Husbands and Traveling Companions; With a Brief Account of the Manners and Customs of that Nation of Savages, of Whom So Little Is Generally Known*.[1] In his foreword to the 1955 reprint of this volume, editor Carl Coke Rister claims that Sarah Horn and Mrs. Harris were among the first, if not the first, Anglo-American women to be captured and enslaved by the nomadic Comanche Indians:

> For many weary and horror-packed months the Indians
> subjected the two women to every hardship and cruelty
> which their primitive minds could invent, but at last they
> were ransomed by kind-hearted New Mexican traders and
> sent to Missouri via the Santa Fe Trail. While captives, they
> had been forced to watch the warriors impose on their
> children inhuman treatment, from which the babe, and
> later little John, died. So it is small wonder that both
> women, when ransomed, were sadly broken in heart, body,
> and soul and lived but a short time to tell their tragic story.[2]

Sarah Horn told her story articulately. The first days in captivity were a litany of pain; partly her own, but mostly the deep agony of watching the suffering of her two little boys, naked in the burning sun, without food or water, and not being permitted to help them. As they traveled, the Indians joined others of their tribe, and retraced their path to the area where they had captured the women. They encountered the bodies of Horn, Harris and the other murdered men, still in the positions of their deaths. The anguish first suffered by the two wives was repeated as they again saw their husbands' mutilated bodies.[3] On the way, the Indians happened upon other travelers, both Americans and Spaniards, who became victims of the same violence.

Texas historian John Henry Brown notes that the party of Beale colonists had left Dolores on 10 March 1836, four days after the Alamo fell. The Texans' surrender at Goliad was made nine days after their departure. According to Brown: ''These ill-fated colonists knew of neither event. They only knew that the Mexicans were invading Texas under the banner of extermination to the Americans, and they dreaded falling into their hands almost as much as they dreaded the wild savages.''[4] News of the massacre of the Beales Colony men and capture of the women and children did not reach the citizens of Texas because 18 April 1836 was the fifteenth day of the latter's captivity, and ''this being but three days before the battle of San Jacinto, when the entire American population of Texas was on, or east of the Trinity, abundantly accounts for the fact that these bloody tragedies never became known in Texas.''[5]

Sarah Horn relates events that happened on April 18:

> Here the Indians, between three and four hundred, separated into three companies of equal numbers; and although the day was exceedingly hot, they lost no time in collecting their baggage, and started off as though greatly apprehensive of danger. Mrs. H. was now separated from me.
>
> From this camp we travelled with all possible speed until the middle of June. During the whole of this long and painful journey my cup of affliction was not in the least diminished . . . . Much of our way was over rough, stony ground, frequently cut up by steep and nearly impassable ravines, with deep and dangerous fords. At one of these last, with high and rugged banks, my little Joseph slipped off the mule into the water, as the creature was struggling to ascend

the uneven bank. The boy behind whom he rode was very
cross, and would not suffer him to hold on . . . . I had just
gained the shore, and turning round saw the child in his
endeavors to extricate himself from his perilous situation.
He had nearly succeeded, when one of the savages, enraged
at the accident, stabbed the little creature in the face with
his lance, and sent him back into the midst of the foaming
stream. The wound was inflicted just below the eye, and was
a very severe one. None of them offered the least assistance,
but seemed to exult in the scene before them; but the poor
suffering little creature made another effort, and, with the
blood streaming down his naked body from his wounded
face, gained the shore. On this occasion the feeling of the
mother triumphed over every other consideration, and I up-
braided the wretch for his cruelty. But bitterly did he make
me pay for my temerity, when with true savage dignity he
made the child go on foot all the rest of the day and drive a
lame mule, with the blood streaming from every part of his
naked and lacerated body. When we halted for the night,
the savage, seated on his mule, called me to him. As I approached him in obedience to his lordly command, he held
his whip in one hand, and drew his knife with the other.
But the deadly steel had no terrors for a miserable wretch
like me; I felt that the bitterness of death was past. With his
whip he gave me many cruel stripes . . . . When the savage
monster had done whipping me, he took his knife and
literally sawed my hair from my head. It was quite long, and
when he had completed the operation, he tied it to his own
as an ornament, and I suppose he wears it yet . . . .

The following day we came to a deep, rapid stream. The
mules had to swim, and the banks were so steep that we had
to get off into the water to enable them to ascend to the
shore. We soon came to the foot of a mountain . . . when we
had reached the summit, we made a halt. A number of the
Indians then took my children and returned with them to
the stream we had just passed. They were absent about an
hour, when I saw them at a distance returning, holding the
children up by their hands; and I observed that when they
let go of them, which they did several times, they fell as
though they were dead. On their arrival at the camp, they

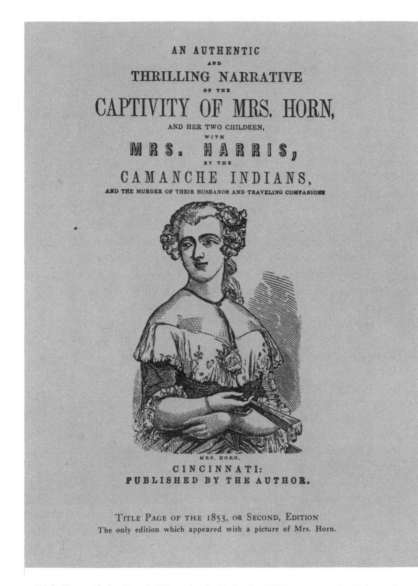

AN AUTHENTIC
AND
THRILLING NARRATIVE
OF THE
CAPTIVITY OF MRS. HORN,
AND HER TWO CHILDREN,
WITH
MRS. HARRIS,
BY THE
CAMANCHE INDIANS,
AND THE MURDER OF THEIR HUSBANDS AND TRAVELING COMPANIONS

MRS. HORN.
CINCINNATI:
PUBLISHED BY THE AUTHOR.

TITLE PAGE OF THE 1853, OR SECOND, EDITION
The only edition which appeared with a picture of Mrs. Horn.

Title Page of the Sarah Horn book. It is the 1853, or second edition, the only one which contained her picture.

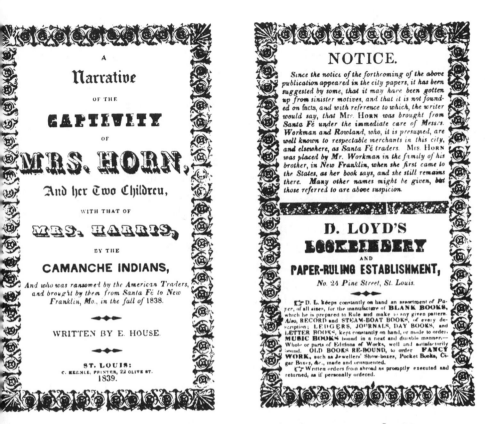

Sarah Horn Book Wrapper. From the original 1839 edition.

were a sight to behold! Their emaciated bodies were enor-
mously distended, and Joseph's face, from the wound he
had received, was dreadfully swollen. They were quite insen-
sible for some time, and the water was discharging continually from their mouth, nose, and ears. The Indians, it
appeared, had been amusing themselves by throwing them
into the stream, and when nearly drowned would take them
out. John was a little more than five, and Joseph less than
four years old . . . .[6]

Later during their wanderings, Sarah Horn saw Mrs. Harris from
time to time and learned her health was precarious. "She was nearly
starved to death; and often has she stole an opportunity to come
to me for a morsel of meat, which she devoured raw, with an
eagerness that indicated that a little longer abstinence would have
relieved her of her woes."[7] However, Mrs. Harris did survive and
was rescued in June 1837. Sarah Horn would not see her again until
they were reunited in Missouri in 1838.

Horn's captivity lasted eighteen months, all spent in nomadic
travels with the Indians. As a slave to a Comanche family, she did
all the menial work and learned to dress buffalo skins. She saw her
beloved sons a few times when they were permitted by their masters
to visit her. The wanderings of the tribe finally brought them to
San Miguel, New Mexico, where she was purchased by a kind
Spanish family.

Not long after, due to some legal manipulations, Horn was
turned over to an avaricious American named Benjamin Hill in
September 1837. He acted little better than the Indians, working
her cruelly and feeding her poorly. She was subsequently rescued
by Mr. Smith, a miner, and stayed with his family until Santa Fe
Trail traders Thomas Rowland and William Workman, upon instructions from William Donoho, arranged for her to go to Taos
in March 1838, where she stayed for six months. Sarah Horn described the change in her life: "In the month of February I received
a present of two dresses, presented by Messrs. Workman and
Rowland, of Taos, with a note, bearing their kind respects . . . . They
commended me to the care of a gentleman by the name of Kinkin-
dall [Kuykendall?], whom they instructed to provide the means and

see that I had a safe conveyance . . . . Friends were multiplying around me . . . and I was favored with the company of a lady, and a Doctor Waldo, as my traveling companions . . . . I arrived at Taos on the 10th of March, and stopped at Mr. Rowlands, and I found him and his amiable lady all I could wish. I spent my time about equally in this excellent family, and that of Mr. Workman.''[8]

The traders and others had searched in vain for her two sons, one of whom was reported dead. When she had given up all hope she finally agreed to go to Missouri. The Rowland-Workman caravan left for the States on 22 August 1838. Sarah was very apprehensive about the trip across the plains: ''Mrs. Harris had left for the States before my emancipation, and I was the only female in a large caravan, united for mutual defense, in traveling across the wilderness a thousand miles, to the western boundary of the United States. The most of this tedious way is infested with hordes of merciless savages . . . . But I felt that now I had but one more life to lose, and should I be deprived of that, it would prove a specific to a wounded spirit.''[9] Sarah would not learn until she reached Missouri that she owed her freedom to William Donoho.

The second capture of a Texas woman occurred in May 1836. Rachael Parker Plummer's tragic tale was made even more moving because she was pregnant at the time of her capture. She would bear her baby in captivity, only to have him murdered by her captors. She would finally be restored to her husband and parents but would die before her little son, James Pratt, was rescued from the Indians.

The story of Parker's Fort is a famous one in Texas lore. This is due mainly to the dramatic story of nine-year-old Cynthia Ann Parker, Rachael's cousin, who was captured in the same raid. Cynthia grew up in captivity with the Indian name Naduah and at an early age became the wife of Comanche Chief Peta Nacona. Her son Quanah was not only the last famous fighting chieftain of the Comanches, but was also the leader who finally brought the Comanches to terms with the white man.[10]

In 1833 a group from the Predestination Baptist Church from Crawford County, Illinois, headed by Daniel Parker, settled near the present town of Elkhart, Texas. Another Parker named John

and three of his sons, Silas, James and Benjamin, preferred to settle farther west, near the Navasota River, where they built a large
stockade of split cedars, buried in the ground three feet and extending up some twelve feet. Two-story blockhouses were erected
at opposite corners, and within the fort were two rows of log cabins.
In March of 1834 the fort was complete and the families of the
brothers, along with other members of the group, moved into the
fort and began clearing land for fields. Life was hard and security
was tight during those early days, but the settlers felt quite secure,
especially since Texas had gained its independence in the battle
of San Jacinto on 21 April 1836.[11] A month later the fort was over-
run and destroyed by Comanches, many of the farmers killed, and
the lives of several Parkers were changed forever.[12]

The story which Rachael Plummer wrote following her rescue,
*Rachael Plummer's Narrative of Twenty-One Months Servitude as a
Prisoner among the Commanchee Indians*, issued in Houston in 1838
and printed by the Telegraph Power Press, is the first story of an
Indian captivity printed in Texas. Conjectured to exist by Texas
bibliographer Thomas W. Streeter, a copy was not discovered until
after his death in 1975.[13] Reproduced in 1977, it differed considerably from both the second, "revised and corrected" edition
published in 1844 in St. Louis and the 1926 third edition published
by descendants of Rachael Plummer. The original story was only
sixteen pages long, contained no dialogue and few geographical
references. The second edition was twice as long and always appended to Rachael's father's *Narrative . . . of James W. Parker*.[14]
Although Streeter believed Rachael had written both narratives,
it appeared that considerable editing and polishing were made to
the second one, possibly by James Parker.[15]

Rachael Parker may have been still in her teens when she married L. T. M. Plummer. They had an eighteen-month-old son
named James Pratt and Rachael was pregnant with her second child
when the raid occurred. Most of the men in the settlement were
working in the fields when the band of Indians appeared on 19
May 1836, asking for beef. Rachael's Uncle Benjamin attempted
to parley with them, but the effort was futile. In her 1838 narrative
Rachael writes:

Quanah Parker next to a painting of his mother, Cynthia Ann Parker, circa 1890. She was a cousin of Rachael Parker Plummer and remained in Comanche captivity for twenty-four years. Photo by H. P. Robinson, Ft. Sill, O. T. Courtesy Archives and Manuscripts Division of the Oklahoma Historical Society, photo number 705.

> I ran out of the Fort by a small back gate that led im-
> mediately into the farm; as soon as I passed the corner of
> the Fort I was again in sight of the Indians, and I saw them
> stabbing their spears into uncle Benjamin and shooting him
> with their arrows . . . one large sulky Indian picked up a hoe
> and knocked me down. I well recollect their tearing my little
> James Pratt out of my arms, but whether they hit me any
> more I know not, for I had swooned away . . . . The first
> thing I recollect was the Indians dragging me along by the
> hair of the head . . . they commenced whipping me in such
> a manner that the wounds and bruises were not well for
> some weeks, in fact my flesh was never clear of wounds from
> the lash and bruises from the clubs, etc. for thirteen
> months, and to undertake to narrate the sufferings I en-
> dured . . . would be utterly impossible.

Later Rachael's hands and feet were tied and she was left facedown,
unable to turn over.

> It was with great difficulty that I could keep from
> smothering in my blood, for the wound they gave me with
> the hoe; and many others, was bleeding freely. I could hear
> my little James Pratt crying for mother, and I could easily
> hear the blows they gave him, and sometimes his feeble
> voice was weakened by the blows. I leave my reader to reflect
> what were my feelings — such horrid undiscribable [sic]
> yelling . . . while dancing round the scalps; kicking and some-
> times stomping the prisoners, who now amounted to five in
> number, viz: Elizabeth Kellogg, widow, uncle Silas Parker's
> oldest daughter Synthia [sic] Ann, aged about eleven; his
> oldest son John, aged about nine years, my little son James
> Pratt and myself.

Rachael saw her child once after their capture. He was brought to
her to nurse, but when the Indians discovered he was weaned, they
took him away. She notes sadly: "This was the last sight I ever had
of my little James Pratt — where he is I know not."[16]

The nomadic wanderings of the Comanches began. After the
tribes reached the plains, the captives were separated, Rachael's
aunt Elizabeth going with one tribe, her cousins Cynthia and John

to another, and she with a third. As the months passed, Rachael's duties were to mind the horses and to dress buffalo skins. Nothing in her story indicates the pending birth of her child until she writes: "About October I was bro't to bed — my little infant, tho' very small, was very pretty and bid fair to do well. I called him Luther T.M. Plummer, for his father." [17] Interestingly, the first and second accounts of the narrative differ considerably here. In the second she recounts: "In October I gave birth to my second son. As the to the months, &c. [etc] it was guess work with me, for I had no means of keeping the time. It was an interesting and beautiful babe." [18]

Not long after, the baby was brutally killed. Rachael's 1838 story gives an immediate sense of impact to the horror:

> He was about six weeks old, when I suppose they thought it was too much trouble, five or six sturdy Indian men came where I was suckling my little infant; one of them caught it by the throat and choked it till it was black in the face and while he was so doing the rest of the Indians were holding me, to prevent me from trying to relieve the child. At length they pulled it from my arms by force — threw it up in the air and let it fall upon the frozen ground until life was, to all appearances, entirely gone!!! They then gave it back to me. I tried to recover it and as soon as they saw that it had recovered a little, they treated it as before several times, then they tied a thong round its neck and threw it in- to the large hedges of prickly pears, which are ten or twelve feet high; they would pull it down through the pears . . . several times; they then tied the end of the rope to their saddles and would drag it round me. When entirely dead, yea, literally torn to pieces! one of them took it up by one leg and brought it to me, and threw it in my lap. But in praise to the savages, I must say they gave me time to dig a small hole in the earth and deposit it away. I was truly glad when I found it was entirely over its sufferings. I rejoice now to reflect that its soul is now in the sweet mansions of eter- nal day. [19]

In March all the Comanche tribes assembled for a war council. Rachael notes: "This was done on the heads of the Arkansas and

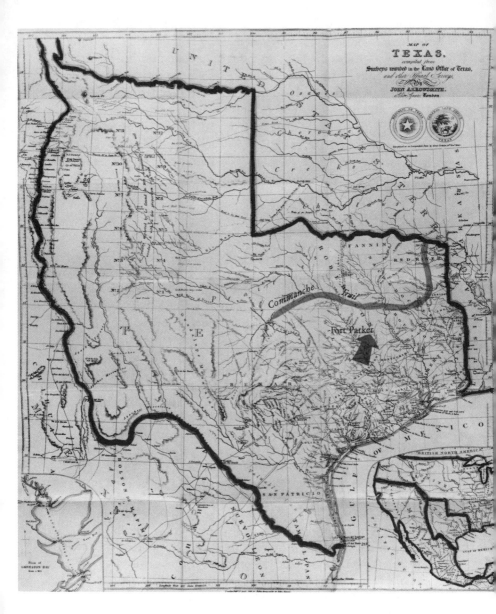

1841 Map of Texas. Fort Parker, where Rachael Parker Plummer was cap-
tured, and a Comanche Trail are marked on the map. (It is also from the
Kennedy book).

it was the greatest assemblage of people I ever saw.'' She had by
this time learned their language and was determined to know the
result of the proceedings. She listened even though she was whip-
ped for it. The tribes devised a great plan to drive the whites out
of Indian country during the coming year.[20]

In June Rachael's deliverance came. Some Mexican traders
arrived. Rachael writes in 1838:

> Hope once more blazed up. I thought perhaps they might
> buy me. We were now, I think, about five hundred miles
> north of Santa Fe. The traders made an offer for me which
> my owners refused — they still offered more, and my owners
> still refused,at length they succeeded in buying me — Oh
> joy that mortal tongue can never tell! . . . This was the 19th
> day of June 1837 . . . . The next morning my new master
> told me he was going to take me to Santa Fe. We started,
> and on the evening of the seventeenth day we reached our
> destination. Language cannot express my feelings, when I
> found myself surrounded by sympathizing Americans, clad
> in decent attire.[21]

Here again, Rachael's two accounts differ. The first is brief and
terse, the second more informative and filled with praise for the
man who provided her ransom and sent the Mexican traders to
rescue her. In the latter she writes:

> I was soon conducted to Col. William Donoho's
> residence. I found that it was him who had heard of the
> situation of myself and others, and being an American in-
> deed, his manly and magnanimous bosom, heaved with
> sympathy characteristic of a Christian, had devised the plan
> for our release [Mrs. Harris had also been purchased by his
> arrangements]. I hope that every American who reads this
> narrative may duly appreciate this amiable man, to whom
> under the providence of God, I owe my release. I have no
> language to express my gratitude to Mrs. Donoho. I found
> in her a mother [there was scarcely a decade difference in
> their ages], a sister to condole with me in my misfortune . . . .
> A friend? yes, the best of friends; one who had been blessed
> with plenty, and was anxious to make me comfortable; and

Reconstructed Fort Parker, Texas. Where Rachael Parker lived when she was captured by the Comanche Indians in 1836. Now a State Historic Site, it is located between Groesbeck and Mexia, Texas. Photo by the author.

one who was continually pouring the sweet oil of consolation into my wounded and trembling soul, and was always
comforting and admonishing me not to despond, and
assured that every thing should be done to facilitate my
return to my relatives; and though I am now separated far
from her, I still owe her a debt of gratitude I shall never be
able to repay but with my earnest prayers for the blessing of
God to attend her through life.[22]

This second, more emotional tribute to the Donohos may have
been embellished by her father, James Parker. If so, the information was undoubtedly garnered from their conversations together
after her return to Texas. Rachael's account also disagrees with James
Donoho's letter, in which he claims his father "went himself after
Mrs. Plummer and Mrs. Harris, and had to carry with him some
of my mother's clothes for them to put on."[23] This information
was obtained from James' elderly aunt and uncle in Missouri fifty
years after it happened and could have become confused. William
Donoho may have gone himself for Mrs. Harris, but it appears
Rachael was brought to him.

In her first version, Rachael Plummer does not mention the 1837
rebellion in Santa Fe when the citizenry rose up against Governor
Perez. It is included in the second edition:

But for the kindness of Mr. and Mrs. Donoho, I would
not have got along. Soon after I arrived in Santa Fe, a distur-
bance took place among the Mexicans. They killed several of
their leading men. Mr. Donoho considered it unsafe for his
family, and started with them to Missouri, and made me
welcome as one of the family.[24]

Return to Missouri

Mr. Donoho, in company with his wife . . . conveyed Mrs. Plummer . . . and Mrs. Harris, from Santa Fe to Missouri in the autumn of 1837. He escorted Mrs. Plummer to her people in Texas.
— John Henry Brown, *Indian Wars and Pioneers of Texas,* 1890s

*I*f the Donoho party left Santa Fe around the end of August, they probably reached Missouri in mid-October. They went first to Independence, where they may have had friends or relatives with whom they could have stayed for a time. James Donoho claims, however: ''They both [Plummer and Harris] returned to Mo. with my father and mother, and all went to the home of my grandmother, Mrs. Lucy Dodson of Pulaski County.''[1]

Rachel Plummer recounts in her 1838 edition how: ''We arrived safely at Independence, in Missouri, where I received many signal favors from many of the inhabitants, for which I shall ever feel grateful. I stayed at Mr. Donoho's, but I was impatient to learn something of my relatives.''[2] It took four months to succeed in locating Rachael's family. On 20 January 1838, the following notice, perhaps placed by Donoho, appeared in the Houston newspaper, *Telegraph and Texas Register:*

> December 1837. Mrs. Plimmer [sic] from Robertson's Colony, Texas was lately purchased from the Comanche Indians, she is at Independence, Missouri. She states she has 3 children and one

sister yet with the same tribe. The above named lady has red hair. For Information apply to Wm. T. Smith, Columbia, Boone County, Mo. Mrs. Harris has been likewise purchased from the Indians and can be found at the same place. She was also taken from Texas.[3]

Rachael only had one child with the Comanches, but her cousins Cynthia and John Parker may be the other children referred to. The William T. Smith mentioned may have been a man of the same name, who with Donoho, would sign the mule transfer document between Luis Lee and Julian T. Smith later in Santa Fe in August. He could have been a trader whose home base was Boone County and he offered to be the contact person for Rachael and Mrs. Harris. The fact that Rachael also had red hair is interesting to note and may have given her a comforting feeling of kinship with Mary Donoho.

John Henry Brown writes: "Mr. Donoho, in company with his wife — a lady of precious memory in Clarksville, Texas — conveyed Mrs. Plummer . . . and Mrs. Harris, from Santa Fe to Missouri in the autumn of 1837. He escorted Mrs. Plummer to her people in Texas."[4] Once he returned the women captives to civilization, William Donoho could have felt his duty was done. However, he was determined to take Rachael to her family, and it took precedence over his need to return to Santa Fe to arrange his affairs there. There is no question that he was a man of great compassion, or in John Henry Brown's flowery Victorian prose of the day, "a lion-hearted, noble-breasted man."[5] Though temporarily secure with the Donoho family, Rachael agonized about getting back to her family. Her stress was evident when she wrote: "My anxiety grew so high that I could not sleep. Every evening I made it my invariable rule to pray, mingled with my tears, to the Almighty God to interced [sic] for me, and in his providence to devise some way for me to get to my people. I was often tempted to start out on foot."[6]

Word of the Houston newspaper story evidently reached Parker's Fort because a month later one of Rachel Plummer's relatives appeared at the Donohos' door. Her account was joyful:

It was now in the dead of winter, and no prospect of getting to my relatives . . . . I walked to the door, and oh joy unspeakable! I saw my brother-in-law, L. D. Nixon. I tried to run to him but was not able. The first question I asked was, is my husband and father alive? — He answered in the affirmative. Is mother and the children alive? — Yes. Every moment was an hour, and it was now very cold weather, but I thought I could stand anything if I could only get started towards my own country. Mr. Donohoe [sic] let me have a horse to ride, and finally we started — Mr. D. accompanying us. We had a long and cold journey and on the 19th day of February, 1838, I arrived at my father's house, where I found my husband and friends all in good health.

I am now once more in the company of dear father and mother and other friends, and moreover have the great pleasure of embracing my beloved husband. But oh! dreadful reflection, where is my little children? One of them is no more — I buried its bloody body in those vast regions of prairies — but I hope its soul is now in Heaven. My body is covered with scars which I am bound to carry to my grave; my constitution broke — but above all and every trouble which haunts my distracted mind is: WHERE IS MY POOR LITTLE JAMES PRATT![7]

On 2 March 1838 the *Telegraph and Texas Register* reported Rachael's return announcing that she had written "a narrative of her adventures, which will be presented to the public in pamphlet form in the course of a few weeks."[8] In the preface of that first edition, Rachael noted, "I had written this narrative partly in Santa Fee [sic] and partly in Missouri, and completed it at my father's in Texas." The preface was written at Parker's Mill in Texas, Montgomery County, 23 September 1838.[9]

Rachael Plummer apparently had a premonition of her own death when she wrote in the preface to the second edition of her story: "I submit the following pages . . . feeling assured that before they are published, the hand that penned them will be cold in death." Rachael died 19 February 1839, exactly a year from the day she arrived at her parent's home, and the book's publication date is listed as "December 3, 1839, City of Houston, Texas."[10] Her father, the Reverend James Parker, wrote, ''She often said that this life had no charms [chains?] for her, and that her only wish was that she might live to see her son restored.''[11]

Rachael's wish was not realized. Four years after her death James Pratt Plummer and his cousin, John Parker, were restored to Reverend Parker on 15 January 1843, having spent seven years in captivity among the Comanches.[12] Another seven years later, when James Plummer was a little over fifteen years of age, on 29 November 1850 a bill was introduced in the Senate of the Texas Legislature ''for the relief of James Pratt Plummer.'' Such bills were required to be read three times, but on the motions of two senators, the rules were suspended and the bill was passed.[13] It did not say whether he received land or money.

As William Donoho was traveling through Texas, either to or from Parker's Fort, one of his stops may have been in Clarksville, and very likely the information he gained there influenced his decision on where he and his family would settle the following year. But for the time being he returned to his family at his mother-in-law's home in Pulaski County and made plans to leave for Santa Fe. Because of the uprising the previous year, information on the 1838 caravan is scant, but he definitely was in Santa Fe by August 8 because he and William T. Smith witnessed the document on the mule.

When Donoho reached Santa Fe, Sarah Horn had left Taos for Missouri, arriving at Independence on the last of September. ''Six days after,'' she wrote, ''I arrived at the house of David Workman (a brother of my kind friend William Workman), New Franklin, Howard County, Missouri, and beneath whose hospitable roof I have since continued to share the kind attentions of him and his amiable lady.''[14] In the meantime, after closing his business in Santa Fe, Donoho left the place permanently and rejoined his family at Mrs. Dodson's. Sarah ''did not know to whose noble act she owed her release,'' but she then met Donoho for the first time and remained several months with his family.[15] She still saw little of him because he was frequently absent on business. The exposures and abuse undergone during captivity soon caused Sarah Horn's death, while she was visiting some friends in an adjoining county.[16]

Mrs. Harris stayed at Lucy Dodson's for less time than Sarah Horn. According to John Henry Brown: "Mrs. Harris had relatives in Texas but shrunk from the idea of going there; and hearing of other kindred near Boonville, Missouri, joined them."[17] She too soon succumbed from the same causes that killed Sarah Horn.

Lucy Dodson and the rest of the Dodson family were apparently very supportive of Donoho's rescue efforts. James writes, "My relatives attest that they (these restored captives) were ladies in the highest sense of the word." Both William and Lucy Dodson, Mary Donoho's brother and sister, were still unmarried when Mary returned from Santa Fe and possibly still living with their mother. Lucy would marry John G. Estes in June before Mary and William moved to Clarksville in October 1839.

Mary's father James Dodson had died in 1832, but his estate was not probated until after Mary and William returned to Missouri. On 6 July 1839, her mother, Lucy Dodson, as principle, and her brothers William and J. N. B. Dodson, as securities, filed a probate document stating the value of the estate at $14,000.[18] Mary drew some slaves from the estate of her father and they were taken with the family when they moved to Texas in the fall of 1839.[19]

All three of the women whom William Donoho helped free from captivity — Rachael Plummer, Sarah Horn, and Mrs. Harris — died within a year of their return. Each was between twenty and thirty years of age. No obituary has been found for any of them.

William and Clarksville

*One of the early settlers of Clarksville was one William
Donoho . . . . He founded at Clarksville in 1842 what is long to
be remembered, the Donoho Hotel.*
— Pat B. Clark, *The History of Clarksville and Old Red River
County,* 1937

When Bright Ray was writing his *Legends of the Red River
Valley* in 1941, there would still have been old-timers
around who recalled stories about the pioneer settlers
in Clarksville. As is often the case, the stories had probably been
handed down through several generations and some of their accuracy was lost along the way. So it was with the Donohos, about
whom Ray writes:

> In the early 1830s an Indian trader and freighter passed
> through Clarksville. He was from Santa Fe, New Mexico, and
> was acting as guide to a party of travelers en route to Fort
> Parker, Texas. Obviously he liked the Red River country for
> when he returned to the ancient city of the Holy Faith and
> the near-by Indian village of Taos, where he also went often
> to trade, he made arrangements to take his family to the
> valley of the Caddos, the plains of the Rio Roxo of the
> Spanish. In 1839 he arrived to cast his lot with the people in
> this wooded, fertile valley. Perhaps the secluded peace of its
> woods appealed to him after the high mountains and
> plateaus of New Mexico. At any rate he dropped from an
> altitude of 7000 feet to a low of 500 feet and liked it. He

watched the immigrants streaming into the new republic.
He saw a big opportunity for trade with little competition.
He established the Donoho Hotel. The man was James
Donoho.[1]

Of course the man was William Donoho, not James, and his trip
to Fort Parker was to take Rachael Plummer home in 1838, not the
early 1830s. Otherwise, Ray's "legend" seems to be fairly accurate.

It is very likely that either on the way to Parker's Fort or on the
return trip Donoho stopped in Clarksville to visit with William
Becknell, now known as "Father of the Santa Fe Trail." Becknell's
last journey on the trail was in 1826, so they could not have known
each other on the trail, but undoubtedly Becknell would have extended hospitality to a fellow trader. He had settled in Clarksville
in 1835 and built a large home on Becknell's Prairie.[2] Becknell
might have encouraged Donoho to settle there and the latter may
have felt opportunity beckon as he observed the infant town and
saw a need in the future for a hotel in Clarksville.

In 1899 James Donoho gave a rambling interview about the early
days to the *Clarksville News*, a short-lived newspaper of which few
issues exist. James' recollections contain some fine history of the
early town of Clarksville and his arrival there. He recalls: "We came
in ox and mule wagons by way of Fort Smith and Fort Towson. There
was little or no town here then, only a few scattering [sic] houses.
My father first rented a double-log house from Mrs. Gordon . . . .
It was two stories high — the upper one having a plank or pun-
cheon floor, the lower floor being native earth — in fact, in those
days the 'ground floors' were literally and truly 'ground floors.'"[3]
Because James was only five months old when his family left Santa
Fe, he had no knowledge of the earthen floors in the old Fonda,
but they were not new to his parents.

> We lived there some three years when my father bought a
> log house from Bob Figures, on the site of where the New
> Donoho hotel now stands. This house was then the only
> house on what is now the public square.
>   The nucleus from which the town grew appears to have
> been about the old spring, which was just across the street
> from the present Christian Church building. There were

then several houses about this spring, and also a store, containing a few goods of the commonest sort . . . . Very little farming was done then. My father first opened up a farm somewhere about where Mrs. Pinkie Washington now lives. My father enlarged the house he bought from Figures and engaged in the hotel business.[4]

Three months after William and Mary Donoho arrived in Clarksville, their fourth child was born. Named Lucy D., perhaps for her grandmother, Lucy Davis Dodson, she arrived 15 December 1839. On 19 February 1842 their fifth child, Penelope C., was born. On July 10 of the same year, seven year-old Harriet, the daughter born in Santa Fe, died. The cause of her death is unknown because no obituary was found, but she was the first of many Donohos and their descendants to be buried in the beautiful old Clarksville Cemetery. The Donoho's sixth and last child, Susan M. J., was born 12 June 1844.

Donoho's trail trading and hotel business in Santa Fe must have been extremely profitable indeed because he began buying land rapidly. During his six years in Clarksville, he acquired over 10,000 acres, mostly headrights, land given as a reward to early settlers of Texas and also to those who fought in the Texas revolution. A headright was sometimes as much as a ''league and a labor'' of land, which totaled over 4500 acres. Some of the parcels Donoho bought were a third or a half of a headright.[5]

In the 1840 tax rolls of Texas, William Donoho is listed as owning three slaves and eight work horses. No doubt the slaves were the ones Mary inherited from her father's estate before they moved to Texas. The Lone Star state was very precise in its tax rates from 1836 on. In 1840 slaves between the ages of fifteen and fifty were taxed at a rate of $3 per year for each one. Four of every owner's workhorses were exempt but William's other four were taxed at twenty-five cents per head.[6] Donoho bought another slave on 9 September 1841, a Negro named ''Guy,'' forty-five years old and ''sound in body,'' for $350.[7]

On 25 January 1840, Donoho made his first purchase of Texas land from John Boon for $500. In the document Boon stated that it was ''400 acres of my headright of a third of a league.''[8] One month later he bought another 450 acres of the same headright from Boon, paying $2000, almost four times as much as the first piece cost.[9] Among many other purchases of land that same year was 640 acres in April on the waters of the Cypress River for which Donoho paid $1000 to Jonathon Bohannon and 880 acres on Boggy Creek from Needham Boon in August.[10] These and many other entries in the deed records of Red River County tell a colorful tale. By the time he died in 1845, William Donoho owned not only the 10,000 acres in and around Clarksville, but also some lots in town.

Apparently William Donoho's efforts on behalf of the women captured by the Comanches came to the attention of the Texas Legislature soon after his arrival in Clarksville. On 17 February 1841 a notice appeared in the Houston paper regarding the ''Acts and Joint Resolutions of the Fifth Congress of Texas.'' It noted that an act for the relief of William Donoho had been passed.[11] However, there may have been others.[12]

In 1843 William Donoho joined a small sheep business. He entered into an agreement with John Mills, whereby sixty-three head of sheep, including twenty-one ewes, were put into Donoho's care for three years. At the end of that time one-half of the increase of sheep and one-half the shearings of the whole flock would be his.[13] There is no record on the outcome of the venture.

The most important enterprise by far was the Donoho Hotel. He was only involved in its operation for three years until his death, but it was an extremely successful business throughout Mary Donoho's life. The building was added onto more than once and was almost completely rebuilt in 1881.[14] By the time Mary turned over the management to her son James late in her life, the hotel had become something of a legend in Texas. In addition to serving as a hostelry, during the Civil War it was the stagecoach stand for Clarksville. In 1965 a historical marker was installed on the town square by the State Historical Survey Committee which commemorated the stagecoach operation. The text reads:

> Across the street from this site and facing the County
> Courthouse which was later (1885) torn down, the Donoho
> Hotel and Stage Stand operated during the Civil War,
> 1861-1865. Travel in those years was heavy, soldiers arriving

in Texas from Arkansas Indian Territory for elsewhere would catch the stage here for home. Many called by to give news to the Clarksville "Standard," one of fewer than 20 Texas papers to be published throughout the war. The "Standard's" emphasis on personal news from camps was valued by soldiers' families.

Stagecoach passengers for Marshall left 4 a.m. Monday, Wednesday and Friday going by Daingerfield and Jefferson, where steamer connections could be made. Railroad and stage connections were made at Marshall, 42 hours after the coach left here.

The stage to Waco every second day went by Paris, Bonham, McKinney, Dallas, Waxahachie and Hillsboro, arriving in 4 days, 14 hours. Connections made in Waco included Henderson, Hempstead, Nacogdoches and San Antonio.

31 stage lines in Confederate Texas hauled mail, soldiers, civilians. 26 made connections with railroads or steamships, expediting travel.[15]

In a history of the town and Old Red River County, a description of the hotel itself is given in a story about William and James Donoho. Pat B. Clark, a grandson of Pat clark, the founder of Clarksville writes:

> One of the early settlers of Clarksville was William Donoho. He was a man of great sympathy and kind-hearted . . . . He founded at Clarksville in 1842 what is long to be remembered, the Donoho Hotel. He came directly from Santa Fe, New Mexico, where his son and daughter were said to be the first white children born in that town. This hotel was one of the greatest attractions to the traveling public toward the southwest and was spoken of far an wide by all who partook of its magnificient bills of fare and hospitality. After the death of the elder Donoho (William), his wife took over the management of this famous hotel with the help of her son, James B. Donoho, best remembered as the "General" by those who always found it convenient to stop over when the occasion presented itself.

It should be noted here that Pat Clark evidently did not know how old James Donoho was when his father died in 1845. At age eight he could not have been a great deal of help to his mother in managing the hotel. Nevertheless, Clark continues:

> James Donoho was an elegant gentleman, kind and courteous to everybody. He was the one boy in a family that included five sisters. It was said . . . that Mr. Donoho was very particular about the comfort of his guests and in dealing with the public. If any case of conduct did not measure up to the standard of the hotel, this guest was never accommodated in the future. The original hotel faced toward the east with porches running across the entire length of it, a distance in fact of 100 feet. There were porches both to the lower and upper stories. The office and lobby were downstairs in the center. The wash rooms, provided with pitchers and bowls, were just to the left, and the living rooms were to the east of the wash rooms. The dining room was to the west of the wash rooms downstairs. A long bell was mounted in front of the hotel which was rung 15 minutes in advance of a meal. The family living quarters were in the end of the building, three rooms and a back porch being utilized. The kitchen had a large staff of Negro servants at the rear of the dining room. Sample rooms were furnished for traveling salesmen and upstairs quarters for the guests. For some of the many enjoyable entertainments that were had in this historical old building, one could peruse the old *Clarksville Standard* with great pleasure and profit. The parties and balls given at the Donoho Hotel were among the greatest pleasure events in the history of the grand old town.[16]

William Donoho was involved in community affairs in Red River County from the beginning. He had been in Clarksville less than three months when he became part of a committee which petitioned the Congress of the Republic of Texas to establish a new county, part of which would be carved from Red River County. Because it was so large and presented a hardship on residents to travel to their county seat, on 3 December 1840, Donoho, along with fifty-eight other men, ''male voters of twenty-one years or

more and inhabitants of the area,'' signed a petition to establish
Bowie County.[17] In 1842, Donoho was one of seventeen men appointed by Chief Justice J. W. B. Stout to preside at an election
to select one representative from Red River County to the Congress
of the Republic of Texas.[18]

Donoho was also named a local justice and in December of 1842
he was called upon in a murder case. Apparently the defendant,
Doss, was judged without a jury trial. ''Benjamin Blanton,''
reported the newspaper tersely, ''murdered by Mark W. Doss, [who
was] arrested, examined by Justices Willison and Donoho. The
Magistrate directed the prisoner to jail and he was later remand-
ed to prison by Chief Justice.''[19]

From an advertisement in the *Standard* it is apparent that
Donoho was a lover of fine horseflesh. Just four months before his
death, he advertised the services of his champion stallion, ''Duke
Luzborough.'' His pedigree read like a who's who of horsedom:
'Duke Luzborough is out of Mary Grey, got by Jackson's Archy Jr.,
who was by old Archy, his dam by imported Dare Devil, grand dam,
imported Pantaloon Cade, by Wormley's King Herod out of
Primrose by imported Dare, out of Taslus out of imported mare
Soluna, by Godolphin, Arabian. Luzborough, imported, the sire
of Duke Luzborough, was got by Williamsons deep sorrel Andrews
by Eleanor, out of Whiskey, out of Young Giantesa, by old Diom-
ed.'' If that did not impress the horsey set of Red River County,
Donoho's description of the stallion may have: ''Duke Luzborough
is a light chestnut sorrel seven years old this spring, and is sixteen
hands high, and cannot be passed by any horse in the United States
or Texas, for form, or beauty, or muscular power.'' Donoho added
that the Duke's services were at a special price: ''Will stand at my
stable in Clarksville, this season, and will be let to mares at the
reduced price of ten dollars the single leap, and twenty dollars the
season, or thirty dollars to insure a mare with foal.'' Donoho was
willing to take the fee in young cattle, cows and calves, or beef cattle,
at the cash selling price.[20] The records of the Jockey Club in Lexington, Kentucky, do not go back far enough to find the Duke of
Luzborough, if indeed he was of champion stature, but it would
be interesting to know if descendants of the horse exist today.

One of the last services William Donoho performed for his community may have been the 1845 Fourth of July celebration in Clarksville. He was one of several prominent men appointed to make the arrangements, including the ''procuring of orators for the day.''[21]

For some reason, Donoho's obituary did not appear in the paper until six weeks after his death. Charles DeMorse, editor of the *Northern Standard* and a power in the town, ran his paper in his own way. Reporting local news was not high on his list of priorities. Fortunately, there was at least a brief notice of Donoho's death; some obituaries were not reported at all. The notice appeared 12 November 1845: ''Died — In this town on the 23rd of September of apoplexy Mr. Wm. Donoho, aged 48 [actually 47] years. The deceased was a native of Madison County, Kentucky, and had lived in this place since 1839.''[22] John Henry Brown said of him: ''William Donoho, [was] one of those great-hearted, sympathetic men who honour humanity.''[23] His death left Mary Donoho a widow at age thirty-seven, with five young children.

Mary

His wife [Mary Donoho] was a strong and fearless woman, intelligent and practical as well; so were his daughters. They were cut by the pioneer pattern.
— Bright Ray, *Legends of the Red River Valley*, 1941

When William died in 1845, Mary Donoho was thirty-seven years old and had been married for fourteen years. Daughter Mary Ann was almost thirteen, James was eight, Lucy six, Penelope three, and baby Susan fifteen months old. Mary would live another thirty-five years, make all the childrearing decisions and become wealthy by managing her hotel very successfully. But first she had to survive a six-year court battle.

William Donoho died intestate and although he may have been one of the original Texas entrepreneurs, his complicated jumble of properties was difficult to untangle. The six years were filled with interminable delays and it was a long wait before Mary was free from financial and legal worries.

Her first action was on 31 December 1845 when she presented to the court an inventory and appraisal of the Donoho estate which totaled $13,600. However, the final accounting would turn out to be larger. A court document states: "Out of said appraisal there is allotted and set-over to the said Mary Donoho for the use of herself and the children the following property." A list follows of what appears to be the hotel's entire furnishings, valued at under

$500, plus "thirteen hundred and twenty-eight pounds of pork and one hundred bushels of corn for the years provisions." It further states that the same was not subject to sale.[1]

Possibly this food was meant to feed the family, the slaves and guests at the hotel. But Mary also needed money and on January 7 following William's death, a notice appeared in the paper advertising an "Administratrix Sale" by Mary Donoho. It informed the public that on the 23rd and 24th day of January she would offer for sale "all of the perishable property belonging to the estate of William Donoho, deceased, consisting of horses, cattle, sheep, etc."[2] However, not only livestock was disposed of. In the Donoho probate papers, there is a yellowed list of personal items which were sold. It includes many pieces of furniture, two trunks, a gun and one gold watch. The watch was the most valuable item and was sold to a Joseph Glover for $60, which then was a great deal of money. Possibly it belonged to William and had to be sacrificed for the welfare of the family. The statement was subscribed and sworn to before Chief Justice W. B. Stout on 27 January 1846 and bears Mary Donoho's signature. A total of $1786 was realized from the sale.[3]

The number of slaves owned by the Donohos was never clearly defined in William's probate records. Mary petitioned the court to be permitted to sell a female slave named Alley at public auction.[4] A year later she reported that she had "not been able to realise anything on account of the want or invalidity of the title to said Negro." Mary was released from responsibility to the court for the sale of Alley. She then requested permission for five other slaves owned by the estate to remain in her employ and that their services would stand as remuneration for the expense of boarding, clothing and schooling her children, the minor heirs to the estate. The five slaves were Julia, age forty-two, her three children and Martin, a Negro man, age twenty-nine. The request was granted. At this same term of court, in order to satisfy a "deficiency of assets," Mary was ordered by the court to sell four town lots owned by the estate, at public auction at the courthouse door, to the highest and last bidder.[5]

Daughter Mary Ann was seven years old in 1839 when the

Donohos arrived in Clarksville and they may have entered her in Mrs. Weatherred's School, the town's first school for girls, when it opened in 1840. It began on Pine Creek but moved into Clarksville in 1844.[6] In 1842 a public notice advertised that per session of five months, the cost for first class students would be $10. They would be taught ''Orthography (which was really spelling), Orthoepy (pronunciation), Reading, Writing and Definition.'' The upper class students would pay $15 per five month session and the curriculum was more rigorous. Classes included ''Philosophy, Astronomy, Rhetoric, Composition, Logic and Chemistry.''[7] As the younger Donoho girls became old enough, it appears that they attended a school called the Clarksville Female Institute, which opened in 1848.[8]

In 1846, Mary Donoho's first-born was married on her fourteenth birthday to Gilbert Ragin, a prominent local man twenty-one years her senior. He was an established dry goods merchant in Clarksville and had been a member of the ill-fated Snively expedition three years earlier.[9] The marriage lasted until his death eleven years later and produced three children: Mary Zyra, born in 1848; Gilbert; 1853, and Charles, 1857.[10] Zyra died at age fifteen and Gilbert at thirty-four. No information was found about Charles.

Also in 1846, tragedy struck Mary's life once again when she lost a second daughter. At the age of seven, two days before Christmas, Lucy D. died. As with Harriet, no obituary is available, but both deaths could have been caused by any one of the many prevalent childhood diseases of the time. Harriet and Lucy share a slender white marble tombstone at the old Baptist Cemetery which is now known as the Clarksville Cemetery.

It was 1851 before the final settlement of the estate was concluded. It gave half to Mary; the other half was to be divided between the four remaining children. The final accounting listed eleven town lots and over 15,000 acres of land in three counties: Red River, Titus, and Cass. It included the 4600 acres of land given to the Donoho heirs by the Republic of Texas, presumably for William's rescue of the three women captives of the Comanches in 1837-38. It was valued at $800, which would have been only about eighteen cents per acre and probably was the land in Montague County which descendants would ask about in 1930. The remainder, over 10,000 acres, was acquired by Donoho in his six years in Clarksville. It included "3977 acres surveyed in the name of William Donoho lying in Cass County," valued at $1 per acre.[11]

Only five slaves are accounted for in the probate document. The Negro man named Martin is listed at a value of $900. He was worth more than the 4600 acres of land in Montague County. The female slave Julia was listed at $550 and her three daughters, Matilda, age 6, Carolina, 4, and Clarisa, 2, had written worths of $325, $250 and $200.[12]

It seems likely that Mary had other slaves because shortly after the estate was settled, she was one of the parties in a sale involving "one Negro woman named Sally Ann, aged about twenty-two, and her three children, Elizabeth, aged six years, a girl about four years and a boy Robert, aged about one year."[13] Five days later, a conveyance on a Negro named Marcus was made, with a notation "to perfect the title to slaves Sally Ann and children."[14] Twenty years later a Robert Donoho married an Ann Caton in Clarksville.[15] Caton was the name of another large land and slave owner. Ann may have been one of his slaves and by then, 1871, she and Robert were free and could marry.

Some of Mary's slaves may have been those she inherited from her father and might not have been included in the estate. By the time the 1860 census was taken, Mary was the owner of fifteen slaves, which was a goodly number, but not large in comparison with others in Clarksville. According to the 1860 Slave Schedule of the U. S. Census, the largest single slaveowner in town was a farmer named Hugh Rogers. He owned ninety-four slaves and had ten "slave houses."[16]

Of Mary's fifteen slaves, five were ten years old or younger. There were six older females ranging in age from twelve years to fifty. Four males were ages twenty to forty-three. The dignity of names was not given for slaves on the schedules, only age and sex. Three slave houses were listed for Mary, but some of her slaves may have had living quarters in the hotel.[17] It is known where the slaves of hotel guests were housed. One account describes "the barn back of the Donoho Hotel where slaves of the hotel guests were always quartered."[18]

The forty-three year-old black male on Mary's slave schedule may have been one that she brought from Missouri. A year after her death in 1880, a former slave of hers died in Clarksville. The story said, ''Mort Donoho, a colored man well known here died on the 30th. Mort was . . . an energetic and industrious man. He was over 60 years old and had been in Clarksville about 40 years, being formerly the slave of Mrs. M. Donoho for whom he had a great attachment.''[19]

If any of the Donoho slaves have carried the name down to the present time, they are not now in the Clarksville area. The name spelling varies slightly, but possibly the little two year-old girl named Clarisa in William's probate document of 1851 may be the same twenty-three year-old Clarissa Donoho who appears on the 1870 census. At that time she had two little boys: William, age three and Jim, six months, but no further information was found.[20]

Mary may have been busy doing some rebuilding on the hotel in 1853. In his 1899 interview with the Clarksville News, James recalled: ''The Donoho hotel that was torn down to be replaced by the present splendid brick, was partially erected in 1853, and was added to later on.''[21] Whether the ''splendid brick'' was before or after 1853 is uncertain, but the hotel definitely was rebuilt or remodeled several times.

It is clear that once William's estate was settled, the hotel thrived under Mary's management. It became renowned among travelers and Mary herself became rather famous as its owner. In the mid-fifties an impressive advertisement appeared in the *Standard*, which had recently changed its name from the *Northern Standard*. Signed by Mary Donoho, it reads:

> Donoho House . . . . This well known Hotel, which has been kept by the present Proprietress for the last seventeen years, has been lately rebuilt and enlarged, until it is now one of the largest and most commodious in the State, affording a large number of single rooms, and ample accommodations for all who may patronize it. It is pleasantly situated on the public square, and is especially a comfortable house. The Proprietress, who returns thanks for generous and continued patronage, flatters herself that long experience in the

The Donoho Hotel. Famous throughout the South for its hospitality and fine food. This photograph was probably taken after it was rebuilt in 1853 by Mary Donoho. Eugene Bowers Collection. Courtesy Anne Evetts. Copy by Sharon Wallace.

business, and an ample corps of assistants and servants, will warrant her in assuring travellers and visitors generally, that their fare and treatment will be satisfactory . . . . A large and well filled stable, a horse lot and carriage house, are attached to the establishment and the horses of travellers will be well fed and attended to.[22]

Mary's claim of being the proprietress for seventeen years is interesting. It suggests that the hotel was her exclusive domain, perhaps while William was spending his time with his thoroughbred horses or making land deals. She might also have run the old Fonda in Santa Fe by herself, while William was off trading in Taos and elsewhere. If this was the case, it reinforces the image of Mary Donoho as an extremely self-reliant and resourceful person. As Bright Ray claims in his chapter on William Donoho: ''His wife was a strong and fearless woman, intelligent and practical as well; so were his daughters. They were cut by the pioneer pattern.''[23]

Itinerant photographers became popular in small towns in Texas in the 1850s. They made the circuit, setting up shop at hotels or other quarters which were readily available to the public. Clarksville was no exception, and Mary Donoho's hotel was where they stayed. Three daguerreotype and ambrotype artists are known to have advertised for customers to have photographs made at the hotel. There were two men: the ''celebrated artist Wooley,'' W. E. Buck, and a woman named Harriet E. Wheat.[24]

Eugene Bowers has sketched the exploits of another ''daguerreotypist'' who had a leaning toward skulduggery: ''Late in May of 1852 one Francis N. Vassallo arrived in Clarksville and registered at the Donoho Hotel, then one of the finest taverns in the state. He informed Mrs. Donoho that he wished to engage board for himself and his horse. He was assigned to a comfortable room and his buggy and horse were taken to the commodious stables of the hotel. At that time a well appointed stable was a part of every first class hotel.'' Vassallo was soon doing a brisk business when a local doctor and pharmacist, Enos S. Look, recognized the possibilities of the new profession and suggested to Vassallo that they go into partnership. Business went along well until an attorney from Houston arrived and filed a writ of attachment to Vassallo's equipment for an unpaid bill of $291. Vassallo skipped town with his horse, buggy and photographic equipment, leaving the doctor holding the bag. ''Dr. Look was one of the signers of a replevy bond and as it turned out the only solvent one . . . Vassallo was a scamp as so many traveling photographers have proved themselves since. . . . He drove out of town headed west and has never been seen or heard of in Clarksville since.''[25]

The social life at the Donoho House is evident from accounts in the newspaper. May Day was an important holiday and Clarksville's two private schools for girls planned special observances. In 1856, following the day-long celebration and the crowning of the queen, the paper reported: "In the evening, we understand that a party was given at Mrs. Donoho's hotel, at which those who wished to join in the festivities of the dance had an opportunity of indulging."[26]

Special entertainment also occurred during the holiday season. 'Christmas Ball — Merry Christmas," is the opening greeting in Mary Donoho's advertisement, which reads: "A ball will be given at Mrs. Donoho's Hotel in Clarksville on the night of the 25th of Dec. Tickets $3 each to be had at the Hotel prior to that time or at the door on the evening named."[27] No doubt antebellum gowns for the women and formal dress for the men were the order of the evening.

A social event in 1856 may have been the catalyst for a romance between a Donoho daughter and a young Clarksville attorney. It was "Examination Week" for the Clarksville Female Institute. The *Standard* editor, Charles De Morse, attended and wrote: "We must bear testimony to the general excellence of the pupils, in the exhibition of their scholastic acquirements." The examinations, piano performances and compositions were followed by oratory from the top students. De Morse praised the guest speaker: "The closing act of the schoolroom exercises was a capital, most appropriate, and eloquent address by our young friend, John C. Burks, Esq." He then rhapsodized about the all night party held at the Donoho House, which was "participated in by a very large and highly delighted company. The small hours of the morning had quietly stolen upon all present, before any dreamed of looking homeward. With the advent of the daylight, joyous hearts were parted, we hope not long, as the several parents carried off their daughters." He added: "We must not omit to mention the very excellent supper set by the hostess of the Donoho House."[28] It is easy to speculate that young Penelope Donoho was smitten by John Burks and his "eloquent address." At any rate, eleven months later wedding nuptials for the young couple would take place.

However, before that occasion, events of a more serious nature intervened. In November 1856 the destruction of the Donoho House by fire was barely averted, and it gave Charles De Morse an opportunity to editorialize for a fire department. Two cabinet shops and their contents were destroyed. "Had the wind continued as it was at the commencement of the fire," warned the editor, "Mrs. Donoho's large, fine Hotel would inevitably have been consumed. The burning of this building would have consummicated [sic] to the Court house and then to the other buildings around the square. Had our town been supplied with a fire engine the fire could easily have been confined .... During the progress of the fire, we were struck with the idea that some regularly organized fire company should forthwith be got up."[29]

The next year Mary moved quickly to quell a new threat to her hotel. "SMALL POX," her notice in the newspaper cautioned: "Understanding that a rumor is abroad to the injury of my house, that a traveler stopped in it affected with small pox and communicated the disease. I wish to state that the person who passed through town a few days ago and has since been taken down with the disease at his house on Pine Creek, did not stay at my house, nor is there any small pox in this house. I give this notice in order that travellers may not be deterred by this report in coming to the Donoho House. [signed] Mary W. Donoho."[30]

Mary's two youngest daughters, Penelope and Susan, at different times married the same man, John C. Burks, the attorney who spoke at their school exercises. But the marriages would bring only tragedy and sadness to Mary. Penelope Donoho was almost sixteen at the time of her marriage on 13 October 1857.[31] Twenty months later she died following childbirth. The obituary appeared in the newspaper six weeks after her death: "Died — Of Puerperal developments, on the 27th day of April, Mrs. Penelope Burks, wife of John C. Burks, Esq., aged 17 years." A flowery eulogy described "the event that has shrouded in gloom the sensibilities of a fond and kind husband, and made desolate and sad the hopes and hearts of a circle of relatives and friends." A second, shorter obituary followed: "On the 3d day of June, the infant son of John C. Burks, Esq., and his consort, the Lady whose death we record above, aged one month."[32]

Just a few weeks before Penelope's death, her husband was named by the governor of Texas to serve as one of three commissioners to determine if land certificates had been illegally issued

Youngest Donoho daughter, Susan Donoho, circa 1859, about age 15. Married shortly after this tintype was made, she died a year later, probably in childbirth. Courtesy Elma Cornelius McWhorter

by the county courts for a development called Peter's Colony and to issue patents on the certificates which were proved legal. The editor of the paper vouched for Burks: "We can speak for the integrity and trustworthiness of Mr. Burks, and have no hesitancy in recommending him to the favorable consideration of those interested in the investigation of Land matters in Peters Colony. He is a regular graduate of the Law Department of Cumberland University, and is well qualified to discharge the duties of the station."[33]

Within four months of Penelope's death John Burks and Susan Donoho were married. Neither the marriage on 1 September 1859 nor her obituary a year later were found in the *Standard*.[34] It seems reasonable to assume that Susan's life was also taken by that killer of women — childbirth. Both women are buried in the Clarksville Cemetery and share a headstone identical to Harriet and Lucy's. There is no mention of the Burks name. The inscription simply reads: "Susan M. J., Dau. of Wm. and Mary Donoho," and her birth and death dates. Penelope's is the same. The most logical explanation is that when James was fulfilling a request in his mother's will that he have "neat tombstones erected over the graves of her five daughters," he elected to have them inscribed with only the Donoho name and not that of their husbands.

Because of the Civil War, one of Mary's brothers, William, and his daughter Lucie came to live in Clarksville.[35] Dr. William Dodson had to resign his chaplaincy in the Confederate Army because of ill health and he joined his family in Texas, where he had moved them after the war began.[36] He set up shop in Clarksville on 13 September 1862 and may have been one of the earliest doctors to practice in the specialty of eye disease. His advertisement on the front page of the *Standard* was headed "OPHTHALMIA," and advised: "The undersigned, having located in Clarksville for the purpose of practicing medicine, proposes to treat those cases of disease of the eyes commonly called SORE EYES in all their forms and grades of violence. WITHOUT PAY UNLESS HE EFFECTS A CURE. Those cases excepted where a membrane have formed over the eyes or vision is impaired or lost by deposits in them."[37]

Dr. John W. Armstrong, Lucie's fiance, was, like his father-in-law, a Methodist minister and an officer of the Confederacy. When he mustered out at the end of the war, the couple was married in Clarksville or Bonham. In July 1866 Dodson and the Armstrongs returned to Camden County to live out their lives.[38]

At the time of the 1860 census Mary Ann Ragin and her children were living at the hotel with her mother and brother James. Mary and Mary Ann could be considered "liberated women" a century before the term was coined. Perhaps because she had seen her mother succeed as a businesswoman, after her own husband Gilbert's death Mary Ann did not hesitate to take over his dry goods business. She advised his customers: "Mrs. M. Ragin would inform the friends and customers of the late Gilbert Ragin, deceased, that the house is again open and will be continued as heretofore, upon the most liberal terms. They are invited to examine the stock and prices, before purchasing elsewhere."[39] A wealthy widow, in 1860 Mary Ann's worth was listed at $32,000.[40] In 1863 she was married again, to widower Captain William Pryor Cornelius. Before marrying Cornelius, she closed out the Ragin business with an auction.[41]

Cornelius, both a farmer and merchant, was another prominent citizen of Clarksville. He was active in local affairs and particularly in Democratic politics.[42] Two children were born to the marriage, Mary Ann Cornelius, known as "Pinkie," and William P. Cornelius, Jr. The nine-year marriage ended in 1872, when Mary Ann died at age forty, the last of the Donoho daughters, and the first Anglo-American baby to travel the Santa Fe Trail. Her obituary reads:

> DIED on Friday, the 16th inst. at her residence in Clarksville, Mrs. MARY A. CORNELIUS. Thus in the meridian of life and in the midst of her usefulness has gone from our midst, to her last resting place, one of those estimable ladies who so much adorn the family and social circle, leaving a vacuum that can never be filled. Death is always an unwelcome visitor, but singularly so in this case. This lady was blessed with pleasant surroundings, a family of little children looking to her for that love, protection and training, which a mother alone can give; and in that family circle, there is a void evermore.

Mary Ann Donoho Ragin Cornelius, circa 1859. About age twenty-seven, from a tintype. Mary Ann was the first Anglo-American baby to travel the Santa Fe Trail. At age nine months she made the journey with her parents in 1833. She died at age forty in Clarksville, Texas. Courtesy Elma Cornelius McWhorter.

Mrs. Cornelius was the daughter of Mrs. Mary W.
Donoho, was born in Columbus, [Columbia] Mo., on the
20th day of October 1832, came to Texas in 1839, where she
has since resided, being in her forthieth year, and having lived in Texas 32 years.

She was a lady of strong intellect, affirmative character,
firm in her convictions, and devoted in her attachments, to
which virtues she added all those graces peculiar to her sex.

To her bereaved husband, whose loss is irreparable; her
aged mother, now afflicted with the loss of her fifth and last
daughter; her affectionate brother, who prided himself upon
the womanly virtues of his only Sister; her absent Son,
whose heart will be wrung with the sad news of her death;
and the helpless little children, who in the future will most
feel their loss; a whole community tender such consolation
as heartfelt sympathy can give in their great misfortune.[43]

The cause of Mary Ann's death is unknown. She too is buried
in the Donoho plot of the Clarksville Cemetery without the Ragin
or Cornelius name on her headstone, only as a daughter of William
and Mary Donoho.

By 1860, when Mary Donoho was fifty-two and her son James
twenty-two, the census listed her as the hotel keeper and head of
the household with a total financial worth of $41,000, about tri-
ple the amount she inherited from the estate. By then James had
begun to build his own fortune, his worth being listed at $6500.
On 20 June 1861 James was married to Virginia Ware.[44] She died
5 August 1863, probably another victim of childbirth, and is buried
in the Shiloh Cumberland Cemetery.[45]

James is highly romanticized by author Bright Ray in *Legends
of the Red River Valley*. In legal documents, newspaper accounts and
his own letters, ''James Donoho'' is always the name used for him,
yet Ray refers to him as ''Jimmy,'' gives him an Irish brogue, and
has him use the term ''Begorrah.'' The fictionalized story may have
been half the result of listening to old timers' tales and half imagination. Nevertheless, his description of the Donoho Hotel seems
quite authentic. The building was not destroyed until the 1940s
so he may have remembered it personally. Ray writes:

Jimmy Donoho grew up in Clarksville, pampered by five sisters and his mother. He had a charm about him that helped to make the hotel popular. When he was twenty-three he joined the 29th Texas Cavalry then being recruited for the southern Confederacy by Captain Charles De Morse, editor of *The Northern Standard* of Clarksville. For nearly four years he was absent from the Red River County capital while his mother and sisters carried on the business at the hotel.

Their business was good at the large, two-storied, two-verandahed establishment on the northwest corner of the Square. There was a thick row of trees in front of the hotel which provided a cool shade for the morning sun, and heat and dust protection in the long summers. Another feature that was familiar to every Clarksvillian and every traveler . . . was a huge iron bell mounted on a thirty-foot pole just outside the entrance. The bell served many purposes, the most popular of which was its loud sonorous call to meals when Mrs. Donoho gave the signal to pull the cord. When Jimmy came home on furloughs from the war there were often extra clangings of the bell.[46]

The remainder of the chapter on Donoho is a litany of his shenanigans in trying to win over a young English girl named Ellen (Nellie) Davies from Canada. She was caught in the drag-net of the Civil War and could not return to her parents in Canada because the blockade had set in. She took a job as a school teacher in Clarksville and waited out the war.[47] James and Nellie were married 26 July 1866, a union which lasted until their deaths nine months apart in 1908. Their first child, Earnest, was born in 1869. According to Clarksville old-timers, he may have been the black sheep of the family. He left town and never returned, but he married and his son, called James B. Donoho, Jr., came to live with his grandfather in Clarksville. Nellie and James' four daughters were: Swan, born in 1871, Mary, 1873, Mattie, 1875, and Nellie, 1879.[48]

The Donoho children were raised in luxury. James and his family had a large home called "The Cedars," with a lake and other amenities. The house was torn down about thirty years ago, but

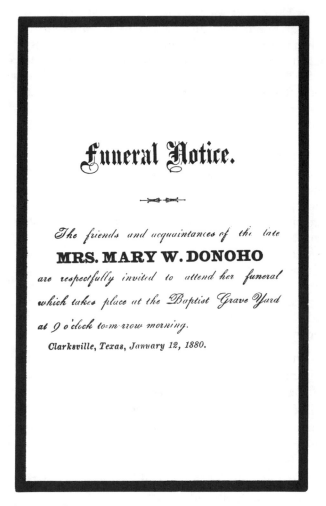

Funeral Notice.

The friends and acquaintances of the late

MRS. MARY W. DONOHO

are respectfully invited to attend her funeral which takes place at the Baptist Grave Yard at 9 o'clock to-morrow morning.

Clarksville, Texas, January 12, 1880.

Funeral Notice of Mary Donoho. All the friends and acquaintances of the deceased were invited to attend the funeral with this kind of funeral card. It was typical of the 1880 era. Eugene Bowers Collection. Courtesy Anne Evetts.

the road which led to it is still called Donoho Street. Mary Kate Hale, a Clarksville old-timer and volunteer at the Red River County Library, writes, "The Donoho family was considered to be aristocratic and cultivated. Their home stood for many years and was very fine for the period."[49]

Mary Donoho's capability as a businesswoman is well documented in the pages of the Red River County Deed Records. Dozens of transactions are in her name either buying or selling land, buying and perfecting titles to slaves, or leasing properties. It appears that she and her family owned a good part of the property around the public square in Clarksville. By 1870, when Mary was sixty-two years old, she may have turned over the management of the hotel to James. He is listed first on the census.[50] Nevertheless, it appears that she retained a good deal of control.

Mary died suddenly on January 12, 1880, at age seventy-three. Her obituary, which contains several errors, corrected below in brackets, follows:

> At the Donoho home in Clarksville on Monday morning, the 12th, Mrs. Mary Wyatt [Watt] Donoho, the daughter of Dr. William [James] and Lucy Dodson.
>
> Her death was painless and without previous illness. Complaining of a difficulty in getting her breath to the question of her son, "What can I do for you?" There was no response and she quietly without a struggle passed away.
>
> The deceased with her husband William Donoho who died in 1845 settled in Clarksville in 1837 [1839], having come from Santa Fe, New Mexico via Missouri. They had moved to New Mexico in 1834 [1833]. Mrs. Donoho was born in West Tennessee, November 24th, 1807, and married in Missouri to which state her parents moved November 7, 1831. Her life had been one of active business until some three years past. She was full of energy and always took interest in all matters of public good. For many years she had been a fervent member of the Baptist Church and felt herself prepared to go at the call of the Great Creator. From her long connection with the Donoho House she was known to great numbers of people in this and other states. She has many relations in Missouri and children and grandchildren

Tombstone of Mary (1807-1880) and William Donoho (1798-1845) in the Clarksville Cemetery. Photo by Sherry Smith.

here who will retain vivid remembrances of her motherly kindness. Always ready, she expected to go suddenly, as she did, having already felt one or more paroxysms of heart disease.[51]

Perhaps because Mary had experienced so much difficulty in the probate of her husband's will, her own was precisely drawn, with no likelihood of difficulties arising. A month after her death in January, her son James, as executor, had filed the probate document. By May, the inventories and appraisals were complete and presented to the court.

Mary's will strongly suggests that she was accustomed to being in control. Throughout the nine pages of the handwritten document, she uses the word ''my'' over seventy-five times. This is illustrated in the paragraph which wills the hotel to James. It reads: "I devise and bequeath unto my said son James B. Donoho . . . my two lots in the town of Clarksville . . . on which my hotel is situated and known as the 'Donoho House' . . . also my Lots No. 7 and No. 8 in Block 11, also my . . . Lot No. 3 in Block 8 being the same on which my stable is situated, now used in connection with my said Hotel." Another item in the will indicates her determination to keep control of her estate in the family. In naming her son James as executor, she writes: "I hereby direct that he shall be required to give no Bond as such Executor and that the County Court shall have no further control over the settlement of my Estate except the probating and recording of this will."[52]

Because Mary survived all her daughters, only James and three grandchildren are named as heirs, her daughter Mary Ann's children: young Gilbert Ragin, Mary (Pinkie) Cornelius and William P. Cornelius, Jr. When Mary wrote the will in 1877, James and his wife Nellie had four children, Earnest, Swan, Mary, and Mattie. Another girl, Nellie, would be born a year later. Only one of the Donoho children, Mary William Donoho, was singled out in the will to receive a specific bequest. Probably she was named for her grandmother and grandfather and was given special treatment because of it. Mary willed to her separately a one hundred fifty-six acre tract of land, "also my dark bay mare about five years old."[53] The grandson and other granddaughters were not mentioned, but Mary indicated that James' inheritance should descend to his lawful descendants in the event of his death.[54]

The inventory of the hotel's furnishings lists ten feather beds, each weighing twenty-five pounds, and valued at fifty cents per pound. Evidently these were considered to be of great value because Mary specifically bequeathed "one of my best feather beds" to each of her three grandchildren: Gilbert Ragin, Mary Cornelius and William P. Cornelius, Jr.[55] The feather beds were to remain in James' possession until each child attained the age of twenty-one. One can only wonder if James saw to it that his own children each got their own feather bed.[56]

The twelfth item in Mary's will reads: "I desire my executor to have neat tombstones erected over the graves of my deceased husband and of my five daughters deceased, the expense to be borne by my estate.'' James carried out this directive, choosing for his father and mother a handsome two-columned marble marker. For his five sisters there were matching single columns in smaller sizes.

Some of the property which Mary bequeathed to her three grand-children was the first land William bought in 1840. It included the piece lying on the waters of Boggy Creek, called ''the Needham Boon tract.'' The number of Donoho acres in Mary's estate were less than when William died in 1845 but the value of the ones Mary kept or purchased in her own right was higher. The land appraisal showed that the Montague County land worth eighteen cents per acre in 1851 had risen to about eight times its original value and was listed at $1.50 per acre in 1880.[57] The final inventory of Mary's estate shows her owning about 6600 acres and eighteen town lots, including the ones on which the hotel was located.[58]

Mary's will states: ''It is my will that after my death my body shall be buried in the Baptist Burial Ground in the town of Clarksville by the side of my deceased husband William Donoho, and in a manner suitable to my condition and circumstances in life.'' Mary Donoho died, as she had lived, a woman of substance.

Donoho Descendants

*When I was growing up, a beautiful old portrait of Mary
Donoho hung in my father's hotel in Crockett, Texas . . . . I will
never forget that in the picture my great-great-grandmother had
red hair.*
— Raymond E. Cornelius, Jr., *Interview, 1988*

*W*hile his mother was alive, James Donoho may have had
to follow her wishes in running the hotel and in other
business matters, but as soon as her estate was settled, he began to do things in his own way. He immediately started
remodeling the hotel and did some traveling. The Donoho Hotel
was made much larger and the *Standard* noted: "The building will
extend to the original stable which has been rebuilt and the entire structure will then cover the north side of the block and will
be 200 feet in length."[1] James expanded his cattle herds, traveling to other counties from time to time to check on them.[2] He
visited Missouri, possibly visiting his Dodson relatives and "bring-
ing back his little daughter who had been at Eureka for sore eyes
and had got well."[3]

James made his visit to Santa Fe in August 1885 as he had resolv-
ed many years earlier. The trip to his birthplace included business
as well as pleasure. When he returned to Clarksville, the *Standard*
reported his visit in detail:

Mr. and Mrs. J. B. Donoho returned from Las Vegas
Springs and Santa Fe, New Mexico, last Saturday. Mr.
Donoho had driven some cattle west and Mrs. Donoho
joined him after the cattle were delivered . . . . Mr. Donoho
was born in Santa Fe, coming here with his parents when
quite small . . . . He presents us with apples from the
Bishop's garden in Santa Fe, also a branch of the pinon with
cones upon it containing the nuts . . . .
They took in the localities . . . and the town of Las
Vegas . . . . He presents us with the publication of the
management giving a view of the grand hotel [the
Montezuma] — lately partially burned . . . . The im-
provements which are the property of the A.T.& S.F.R.R. are
costly and elegant. He showed us photographic views of the
valley adjoining the canon of the Gallinas. The locality is
lovely, the temperature we are assured is delightful.[4]

James and Nellie had a second son, named for his father, in 1877.
He died just before his second birthday according to a tiny stone
in the Clarksville Cemetery which says "James B. Donoho, Sweet
Baby." His death on 30 June 1879 may have been close to the birth
of the Donoho's last daughter Nellie. She is listed as one year old
on the June 1880 census.

"The Cedars," James and Nellie's home on Donoho Street, was
much admired and is still recalled by Clarksville old-timers as one
of the showplaces of the town. As they grew up, his daughters enter-
tained their beaus on the cool veranda, in the spacious gardens,
or by boating on the lake. All of them eventually married.

According to Mary Donoho's great-granddaughter, Elma
McWhorter, the Donoho's oldest child, Earnest, died young and
was buried in Kansas. His wife had died earlier and their son, James
B. Donoho, Jr., came to live with James Donoho by the time he
was six years old. James' second daughter, Mary Donoho Pearson,
was strongly attached to James Jr., and cared for him much of the
time. He was fifteen when James died in 1908. In his will, although
he left his entire estate to daughters Swan, Mary, Mattie and Nellie,
James asked them to "do for James B. Donoho, my grandson,
whatever you four think is right and best, as I have perfect con-

*James B. Donoho and his grandson, James B. Donoho, Jr. In 1898
Donoho was sixty-one years old, his grandson was five. Courtesy Clarksville
Historical Society. Copy by Sharon Wallace.*

fidence in your judgement as to the right for him."⁵ James Jr. served
in World War I and was gassed. It affected his health and he died
in 1925 at the age of thirty-two, having never married. With him
died the last hope of the Donoho name being carried on.

There is little information available on the Donohos near and
after the turn of the century. There are few, if any, extant copies
of the *Clarksville Times*, which began in 1873 and later succeeded
the *Standard* as the town newspaper after Charles DeMorse died.
A fire which destroyed thirty or more years of the paper occurred
before old newspapers were being microfilmed so virtually no
obituaries or other social commentary can be found for the period.
Fortunately, one of the pieces of memorabilia found in her family
papers by Elma McWhorter in January 1991 was the obituary of
James Donoho. It reads:

All Clarksville was plunged into grief yesterday evening a little after five o'clock by the announcement that Captain J. B. Donoho had expired suddenly at his home in the western suburbs of the city. The Captain was in the city both before and afternoon and [was] feeling and looking unusually well, although his general health has been breaking for some time. Last March his wife died and he had a severe attack of grip and has never been altogether himself since.

He was born in Santa Fee [sic], New Mexico, 71 years and six months ago and was brought to Clarksville when a very small boy and has resided here ever since. His parents were successful people before him, and acquired considerable property. This was inherited and well handled by the son and during his time, he was quite a man of affairs.

The Donoho Hotel block was erected by him and associates, as well as quite a number of other brick business houses. In all the affairs of the city he was always liberal and progressive; in fact the city has had few citizens so useful and so universally loved and esteemed.[6]

Some information on the Donoho sisters has been handed down in Clarksville by word of mouth. A Clarksville resident, Ruth McCulloch, age ninety-nine in 1987, still remembers them vividly. She was a younger contemporary of theirs, and spoke with great sadness of the day the Donoho furniture and other belongings were auctioned off in Clarksville. She has much affection for a lovely old chair she bought which had belonged to "Miss Mary."[7]

Swan Donoho, the oldest daughter, married an attorney, Amos Leonidas Beaty, in 1893. He practiced law in Sherman, Texas, until 1907, then in Dallas and Houston until 1913, when they moved to New York City. He served there as general counsel, director and president of the Texas Company.[8] Elma McWhorter recalls that late in Swan's life she and Amos were in France when Swan was killed in an automobile accident. Her body was brought back to New York, where McWhorter believes she was buried. According to Amos Beaty's entry in *Who's Who*, his wife died on 1 August 1930.[9] They had no children.

Mattie Donoho was the only one of the four Donoho girls to bear a child. She married George W. Bayless, with whom she had one son, Benjamin D. Bayless. She died on Christmas Day, 1951, at the Broad Nursing Home in Evanston, Illinois.[10] It appears her ashes were brought back to Clarksville.[11] Records indicate "Mollie Donoho Bayless" is buried in the Clarksville Cemetery.[12] The dates 1875-1951 are correct, so apparently when the stones were inventoried hers was mistakenly read as "Mollie" instead of "Mattie." Her husband died in 1955, also in Evanston.[13] Their son Ben married and had two sons, Ben B. Bayless and George D. Bayless, whose last known addresses were Illinois and Florida respectively.[14]

Nellie Donoho married William C. Hamilton, the leading dry goods merchant in Clarksville. Nellie was very fashionable and active in Clarksville social affairs. In an old photograph she appears in elegant costume for a lavish George Washington birthday gala near the turn of the century. Will died in 1951; her death followed in 1956.

Mary William Donoho, the granddaughter singled out by Mary Donoho in her will, married Dr. Henry Lucius Pearson, a dentist who was fifteen years her senior. Their home and office are still in good repair today and are used as offices by the Beadle law firm. Dr. Pearson died in 1945 at the age of eighty-seven. He left Mary in excellent financial condition, and with some good advice and judicious investments, she tripled her worth.[15] The last of the Donoho children, Mary Pearson died at age eighty-nine.

Problems had developed when Mary Pearson's lifelong attorney moved away and she depended on another, who died. When her own death occurred in 1962, the estate was thrown into chaos because she had made more than one will. Since she had no children, her will directed that a major portion of the estate go to non-blood relatives. Two great-nephews, the Bayless sons, broke the will and, being the two closest blood kin, became the primary heirs.[16] Their representative came to Clarksville and auctioned off all the Donoho belongings, much to the dismay of the old-timers of the town. Whether any heirloom possessions such as photographs were kept by the Bayless sons is unknown and efforts to track them down have been unsuccessful.

Mary Ann Donoho's son Gilbert Ragin married Ella Cheatham in 1879, but he too died young, at age thirty-four. His older sister

Zyra Ragin, who died at fifteen, is immortalized on canvas. A large portrait of her showing a delicate blond beauty hangs above the mantelpiece in the home of Mary Donoho's great-granddaughter, Elma Cornelius McWhorter of Palestine, Texas. A hint of strawberry blond can be detected in Zyra's curls, perhaps a heritage from her red-haired grandmother. McWhorter has an exquisite antique quilt that was made for Zyra with her name and date stitched in the corner. It was 137 years old in 1988. McWhorter also has the only known photograph of Mary Donoho, a tiny tintype measuring less than two by three inches. It came down to her from her grandmother, Mary Ann Donoho Ragin Cornelius, who traveled the Santa Fe Trail with her parents when she was nine months old.

A sister of William Pryor Cornelius, Mary Ann's second husband, married into the Ward family, which was instrumental in founding the Ward Belmont School for young ladies in Nashville, Tennessee. Mary Ann and William's daughter Pinkie Cornelius was sent to the school and when she returned in 1882, the *Standard* announced: "We are glad to welcome Miss Pinkie home."[17] She married M. Starkie Washington, and they lived in her house located on the corner of Donoho and Washington Street. She died in 1942. They had a daughter, also called "Pinkie," who never married and who died in 1973.

William Pryor Cornelius, Jr., attended a military academy in Louisville, Kentucky. He was supposed to enter the U. S. Military Academy, but after discovering he had a hearing problem and could not pass the physical, he returned to Clarksville. During the summer of 1891, a winsome young lady named Imogene Kibbe, of Gainesville, Texas, made an extended visit to friends in Clarksville. Will Cornelius, Jr., began an earnest but proper courtship. In the family memorabilia discovered by Elma McWhorter in January 1991 was an abundance of century-old correspondence, yellowed with age. The letters paint a picture of a warm, close-knit family, beginning with Will's requests for Imogene's company. In those horse and buggy days, formal handwritten notes were the recognized standard of etiquette. Several of Will's courting notes to Imogene survive. Presumably, they were hand-delivered during the afternoon preceding each of his visits to her:

Mr. and Mrs. William P. Cornelius, Jr. Mary Donoho's grandson and Imogene Kibbe were wed in 1891. He served as mayor of Clarksville in later years. They were the parents of Elma Cornelius McWhorter. Courtesy Elma Cornelius McWhorter.

July 23, '91
Miss Imogene,

If agreeable, I will be pleased to call this evening.

Your friend
Will Cornelius, Jr.

A second note reads: "If agreeable, I would be pleased to accompany you for a drive this Evening. Will call about a quarter to seven."[18]

Evidently the young couple had an understanding by August 16. Imogene had returned to Gainesville and Will wrote: "Dear . . . for as long as I am able I am going to keep you from all want and work. It may not be for always, but I will do my best to make it always . . . .[19]

In December the *Gainesville Daily Register* reported: "Married this morning at 8 o'clock at the residence of the bride's parents, Miss Imogene Kibbe and Mr. W. P. Cornelius of Clarksville. The wedding was a very private affair, none but the most intimate friends of the bride being present . . . ."[20]

Will became a successful businessman and later the mayor of Clarksville. He and Imogene lived all their lives there and had five children: Cammie, born in 1892; Rebekah, 1895; William Ragin,

1899; Raymond Edwin, 1903; and Elma Louise, 1905. Of these five, the only descendants of Mary and William Donoho are the offspring of the marriage of Raymond E. Cornelius, Sr.. None of the others had children.

In 1893 Imogene paid a visit to her parents in Gainesville and received a letter from Will: "My Dear Wife, Enclosed find post office order for ten dollars. If this is not enough let me know . . . I am going to have our room paper[ed] and painted as soon as the house is finished. We have got a nice large fireplace in our room and I think it will be a very comfortable house to live in . . . a kiss for you and darling little Cammie. Your loving husband, Will."[21]

An old note in the family papers tells of the purchase of a piano in 1905: "This is to certify that Will and Imogene Cornelius have paid $70.00 (seventy dollars) for the Cornelius piano, paid to Miss Zue Cornelius."[22] This occurred when the four youngest children were ages two to thirteen. Elma would be born three months later. The children who were interested would be given piano lessons.

In the early part of the twentieth century, Clarksville schools went only through the tenth grade, so Cammie, born in 1892, was sent away to Boscobel College in Nashville, Tennessee, for three years. A final year was spent at Ward Belmont School in Nashville. She was thought to have talent in art, so Boscobel was chosen for its well-known art department. The school offered seven math courses including Calculus; six sciences and five foreign languages, but Cammie's most taxing courses were English grammar and general history, for which she received grades of 94% and 96%. Her easier classes included "housekeeping," which earned her a grade of 100%, piano, 90%, and art, 96%.[23] Elma McWhorter, Cammie's youngest sister, recalls that by the time she reached high school and college age, Clarksville offered higher schooling and she was educated there.

Now in Elma's possession, Cammie's horde of letters from the early years indicate she was the letter writer of the family. In a beautiful Spencerian script, her warm and loving missives to her "Mamma and Papa" tell of the many outside activities she and her classmates shared while in school at Boscobel. They attended grand opera, but also enjoyed theatrical performances of lesser stature. In 1913 Cammie writes: " ... We had a real nice Thanksgiving and went to the matinee that afternoon, 'The Trail of the Lonesome Pine.' The scenery was just beautiful. They had a sunset and a sunrise scene that was so pretty ... we enjoyed it all so much."[24]

Even though Texas women were eight years away from full suffrage in 1912, a partisan interest in politics surfaces in one of Cammie's letters: "We were surprised when Roosevelt [Theodore] announced himself for president. I hope he will be beaten worse than Bryan [William Jennings] ever was. I saw in the *Texas Banner* last night that most of the state was for Taft [William Howard] .... Everyone here seems to think that Gov. Hooper will be Gov. for another term. His wife is a graduate of Boscobel ...."[25]

Cammie did not marry. Being a spinster may have heightened her interest in the family history and made her the repository for the family memorabilia. It was on the wall of Cammie's home in Clarksville that Elma McWhorter remembers a large version of the tintype of their grandmother, Mary Ann Donoho Ragin Cornelius, which Elma discovered in her own family possessions in January 1991. A similar episode had occurred in October 1990, when Raymond Cornelius, Jr., of Lufkin, Texas, found a letter in a small black box which had belonged to Cammie, his aunt. Written not long before her death in 1969, it was to his father, Raymond Cornelius, Sr., and reveals that Cammie was well versed in the family history: "Our Great-Grandmother, (the picture you have), Mary Dodson ... married William Donoho. For a while they lived in Santa Fe, New Mexico, where our Uncle Jim Donoho was born."[26] The discovery of this letter confirms that the Santa Fe segment of the Donoho history was known to older members of the family, but simply had not been passed down to the younger descendants. It is the only known contemporary documentation of Mary Donoho's story.

The second Cornelius daughter, Rebekah, attended Ward Belmont School in Nashville and later became Mrs. G. W. Monts. They moved to Colorado where she lived out her life. They had no children. William Ragin Cornelius served in the U. S. Navy in World War II. He was married twice, briefly, but had no children.

Raymond Edwin Cornelius, Jr., the great-great-grandson of Mary Donoho, with his sons, 1981. Left to right, James Stokes, William Ragin, Raymond Edwin, Jr., and Raymond Edwin III. They live in Lufkin, Texas. Courtesy Raymond E. Cornelius, Jr.

He died in 1977 and is buried in the Cornelius plot in the Clarksville Cemetery with his parents and Cammie.

Raymond Edwin Cornelius and his wife Alta owned the historic Crockett Hotel in the town of Crockett. A historical marker has been placed on the site by the Texas State Historical Committee, naming the Cornelius' as the last owners. Their son, Raymond E. Cornelius, Jr., of Lufkin, Texas, recalls: "When I was growing up, every day for the first twenty years of my life I saw the beautiful old picture of Mary Donoho hanging in my father's hotel in Crockett, Texas. It was a large oil portrait, probably done from the little tintype which Aunt Elma has. It must have come down to my father from his father William Cornelius, Jr., because my father understood it had also hung in the Donoho Hotel in Clarksville. The Crockett Hotel burned down in 1974 and the portrait with it. I will never forget that in the picture my great-great grandmother had red hair."[27]

However, one treasured heirloom is still in the Raymond Cor-

Elma Cornelius McWhorter, the great-granddaughter of Mary Donoho, at her home in Palestine, Texas. Born in 1905, she remains very active. Photo by the author.

nelius family. He has a large silver coffee server, believed to be the one used by Mary Donoho in her hotel. Cornelius and his wife Jane have three sons, James Stokes, born in 1957; Raymond Edwin III, 1962; and William Ragin, 1966. Of course William is named for his ancestor. They are the seventh generation since James Dodson and although there are many descendants in Missouri, only the Cornelius name carries on the line in Texas.

At age eighty-three in 1988, Elma Cornelius McWhorter is the last of her generation — the only surviving great-grandchild of Mary Donoho. A sprightly, articulate and gracious Southern lady with a touch of her great-grandmother's red hair, she was excited about the discovery of Mary Donoho. She did not know her ancestor had traveled the Santa Fe Trail in 1833, but there were family stories that someone, possibly her grandfather Cornelius, had rescued a woman from the Indians. Also, there are heirlooms to remind new generations of their heritage. At the end of a hall in her home in Palestine, Texas, stands a massive and magnificent pier glass, almost eight feet tall. Richly carved and with a marble-topped base, it came down to her from the old Donoho hotel. Family tradition says it came over the old wagon road to Clarksville by ox train.

Elma Cornelius was born in Clarksville on 16 June 1905, the day before her grandfather William Cornelius, Sr., died. She recalls her years in Clarksville with genuine pleasure: "I had a grand time growing up there. My father was a wonderful man and we were very proud of him — being mayor of Clarksville and all." She is content with her life in Palestine. Her husband, L. S. "Mack" McWhorter, who was always very active, suffered a stroke in 1987 and was confined to their home. She spent a great deal of time caring for him until his death 1 January 1991. They had no children, but she has many friends and is close to her nephew, Ray Cornelius, who visits frequently.

Elma McWhorter is not at all surprised that it was her great-grandmother who traveled the Santa Fe Trail before any other Anglo-American woman. She is delighted that the information has come to light in time for her to know about it and proclaims: "Nice things have happened to me all my life. Knowing that my great-grandmother was a part of Santa Fe Trail history is another."

Notes

Chapter One — *Discovering Mary Donoho*

1. John Sherman, *Santa Fe: A Pictorial History* (Norfolk/Virginia Beach, Virginia: Donning Company, 1983), 40.
2. *The Santa Fe New Mexican*, 19 August 1885, 4.
3. Sherman, *Santa Fe*, 21: One bit of irony in the story is James' intention to meet with Don Nicholas Pino, the "Sage of Galisteo." Eight years after William Donoho left Santa Fe, Pino was one of those who plotted to overthrow the American government in 1846. After the assassination of Governor Charles Bent by Mexican nationalists and Pueblo Indians in Taos, Don Nicholas swore his allegiance to the United States. He pledged that his family would always serve in the government of New Mexico, and he himself went on to serve in the territorial legislature. (Sherman, *Santa Fe*, 21). It is possible that the elder Donoho was known to Pino, who would have been about eighteen years old in 1837. When James came to Santa Fe, Pino was sixty-six years old. No further account was found in *The New Mexican*, so it may never be known if the two men did indeed meet.
4. *The New Mexican*, 19 August 1885, 4.
5. Letter, James B. Donoho to John Henry Brown, 23 December 1886, Brown Papers, Eugene Barker Texas History Center, University of Texas, Austin.
6. Ibid, 1 January 1886.
7. Isabelle Gordon was the wife of Pat Clark, the founder of Clarksville. She remarried after Clark died.
8. Letter, Donoho to Brown, 5 February 1887.

Chapter Two — *Missouri Beginnings*

1. This is an error. His tombstone reads 29 December 1832.
2. *History of Laclede, Camden, Dallas, Webster, Wright, Texas, Pulaski, Phelps, and Dent Counties, Missouri* (Chicago: Goodspeed Publishing Company, 1889), 899.
3. William H. Whitsitt, *Genealogy of Jefferson Davis* (New York and Washington: The Neale Publishing Company, 1910).
4. "History of Camden County, Missouri," *The Reveille*, 13 August 1896, 3.
5. Nadine Hodges and Mrs. Howard W. Woodruff, *Missouri Pioneers*, "County and Genealogical Record," Vol. XXI, 1973, 56.
6. Walter Williams, *The State of Missouri* (Columbia: Press of E. W. Stephens, 1904), 344.

7. "Auglaize Creek" Card, Ramsey Place Names, Collection No. 2366, 1943, Joint Collection University of Missouri Western Historical Manuscript Collection-Columbia and State Historical Society of Missouri Manuscripts.

8. Fern Moreland, "Glaize City," *Camden County Historian* (Linn Creek, Missouri: Camden County Historical Society, 1982-83), 20.

9. Jacqueline Hogan Williams and Betty Harvey Williams, *Camden County Missouri Tombstone Inscriptions* (Warrensburg, Missouri: n.p., 1968), Vol. I, 61.

10. Moreland, *Camden County Historian*, 20.

11. *History of Laclede*, 292.

12. Williams, *Camden County Missouri Tombstone Inscriptions*, 62.

13. Neva Crane, "The Dodson Family," *Camden County Historian*, 22.

14. *Jefferson City People's Tribune*, 12 February 1868, 2. In this and a subsequent newspaper story Wet Glaize is spelled Wet Glaze. Evidently this occurred frequently, according to the "Wet Glaize" card, Ramsey Place Names Collection.

15. Ibid, 1 April 1868, 2.

16. Rev. William M. Dodson, "Autobiography," *Camden County Historian*, 1982-1983, 23, 24.

17. Deed Records, Boone County, Daniel Boone Building, Columbia, Missouri, 12 February 1833, Book E, 37.

18. Crane, *Camden County Historian*, 22.

19. *The Reveille*, Linn Creek, Missouri, 13 April 1906, 4.

20. *Standard*, Clarksville, Texas, 16 January 1880, 3.

21. Marriage Record, Boone County, Daniel Boone Building, Columbia, Missouri, 119.

22. Polly Donoho Probate Papers, No. 278, Boone County Courthouse, Columbia, Missouri.

23. Ibid.

24. Red River County Probate Records, Clarksville, Texas, Book W, 410-414, 426-429.

25. Deed Records, Boone County, Daniel Boone Building, Columbia, Missouri, 25 January 1839, Book I, 555.

26. Ibid, 22 June 1829, Book C, 291-292.

27. Ibid, 31 January 1833, Book E, 19-20.

28. *Missouri Intelligencer*, Columbia, 8 November 1834, 3.

29. *History of Boone County, Missouri* (St. Louis: Western Historical Company, 1882), 163.

30. Interview with Keith McCann, Camdenton, MO, 12 July 1989. According to McCann, an old-time Camden County farmer and owner of the farmhouse adjacent to the Glaize City Cemetery, at one time there was a burying ground for slaves on the south side of the cemetery fence. He said that many years ago black descendants came to visit, but the headstones slowly disappeared and the graves began to be farmed over. There is no longer a shred of evidence that burials ever existed there. McCann also showed foundations of what was

---

once the blacksmith shop of Glaize City and says the only building which exists today from that early time is a small stone cell back of his farmhouse. The roof and half of the walls are gone, but in one wall there is a tiny window with bars. He says it was used to isolate slaves when the owner decided punishment was in order.

Chapter Three — *Women on the Santa Fe Trail*

1. Susan Shelby Magoffin, *Down the Santa Fe Trail and Into Mexico, The Diary of Susan Shelby Magoffin, 1846-1847*, ed. Stella M. Drumm (New Haven: Yale University Press, 1926; rpt. ed., Lincoln: University of Nebraska Press, 1982), 102-103. Evidently it did not occur to Magoffin to include her maid Jane, who was traveling with them, as "another first American lady to come under such auspices." More than likely, Jane was black and may have been a slave as well. There is no reference in Magoffin's journal verifying this, only that Susan was having difficulties with Jane's insolence, possibly because the maid had been imbibing from the liquor cask. But a fictional account of Magoffin's story says Jane is black and had tended Susan Magoffin from childhood. (Jean M. Burroughs, *Bride of the Santa Fe Trail* [Santa Fe: Sunstone Press, 1984], 7, 8). If Jane was black, she may have been the first woman of her race to travel the Santa Fe Trail to its end. However, she was preceded down the trail as far as Bent's Fort by another black woman. "Black Charlotte" and her husband Dick Green, a slave of Charles Bent's, worked at the fort in the early 1840s. Renowned for her cooking, Charlotte called herself the "only lady in de whole damn Indian country." (David Lavender, *Bent's Fort* [Garden City, New York: Doubleday & Company, Inc., 1954], 160).

2. Josiah Gregg, *The Commerce of the Prairies: or the Journal of a Santa Fe Trader, during Eight Expeditions across the Great Western Prairies, and a Residence of nearly Nine Years in Northern Mexico.* 2 vols. (New York: Henry G. Langley, 1844); rpt. ed., ed. Milo Milton Quaife (Lincoln/London: University of Nebraska Press, 1967), 36.

3. Louise Barry, *The Beginning of the West* (Topeka: Kansas State Historical Society, 1972), 163.

4. Marc Simmons, "New Mexico's Spanish Exiles," *New Mexico Historical Review* 59 (1984): 67-79.

5. Magoffin, *Down the Santa Fe Trail and Into Mexico*, 136. The name is spelled Robidou here. It is generally spelled Robidoux.

6. Rebecca McDowell Craver, *The Impact of Intimacy, Mexican-Anglo Intermarriage in New Mexico, 1821-1846* (El Paso: Texas Western Press, The University of Texas at El Paso, 1982), 30-31.

7. Barry, *The Beginning of the West*, 233.

8. Leo E. Oliva, *Soldiers on the Santa Fe Trail* (Norman: University of Oklahoma Press, 1967), 35-36.

9. *Missouri Intelligencer,* Columbia, 20 July 1833, 3.

10. Barry, *The Beginning of the West,* 233; Oliva, *Soldiers on the Santa Fe Trail,* 36.

11. Barry, *The Beginning of the West,* 234; Oliva, *Soldiers on the Santa Fe Trail,* 36.

12. Letter, Captain William N. Wickliffe to Bt. Major Bennet Riley, 4 August 1833, National Archives, Washington, D. C., Record Group 94, AGO Letters Rec. A-162-1833.

13. Barry, *The Beginning of the West,* 234.

14. *Missouri Intelligencer,* 20 July 1833, 3.

15. R. L. Duffus, *The Santa Fe Trail* (Albuquerque: University of New Mexico Press, 1972), 208.

16. Francis X. Aubry, called "Skimmer of the Plains," was known for his unprecedented speed in traveling the trail.

17. Marian Sloan Russell, *Land of Enchantment, Memoirs of Marian Russell Along the Santa Fe Trail,* Dictated to Mrs. Hal Russell, ed. Garnet M. Brayer (Evanston, Illinois: Branding Iron Press, 1954; rpt. ed., Albuquerque: University of New Mexico Press, 1981), 14, 22.

18. Letter, James B. Donoho to John Henry Brown, 5 February 1887, John Henry Brown Papers, Eugene C. Barker Texas History Center, The University of Texas at Austin.

19. Barry, *The Beginning of the West,* 426-27.

20. Ibid, 572-73.

21. *The Santa Fe Republican,* 21 May 1848, 3.

22. U. S. Census Records, Santa Fe County, New Mexico Territory, 1850.

23. Ralph Paul Bieber, *The Papers of James J. Webb, Santa Fe Merchant, 1844-1861.* Reprint, Washington University Studies, Vol. XI, Humanistic Series, No. 2, 1924, 290.

24. Marian Meyer, "They Were Alone Among the Heathen," *Santa Fe Reporter,* 28 March 1984, 13.

25. U. S. Census Records, New Mexico Territory, Santa Fe County, 1850, 1860, 1870, 1880.

Chapter Four — *The Santa Fe of the Donohos*

1. David J. Weber, ed., *The Extranjeros: Selected Documents from the Mexican Side of the Santa Fe Trail* (Santa Fe: Stagecoach Press, [1967]). The following collections were scrutinized and yielded no mention of the Donoho name: Manuel Alvarez Papers, New Mexico State Records Center and Archives (NMSRCA), Santa Fe; Mexican Archives of New Mexico, 1821-1846 (all documents which included *guias, tornaguias* or contained names of American traders for the years 1833-37; Hacienda Records; Comisaria Substituta and Miscellaneous Records), Rolls 17, 19, 22, 24, NMSRCA; Albert William Bork, *Nueves Aspectos del Comercio Entre Nueve Mexico y Misuri, 1822-46*: Thesis Kue Presenta, Albert William Bork Para Obtener El Grado de Doctor en Letras,. Mexico 1944 (Coronado Microfilm HF 3155 B64, Center for Southwest

Research Studies, University of New Mexico, General Library, Special Collections). Catholic church records were examined because even though the Donohos were Protestant, there was the possibility that the Irish origin of the name could have indicated a Catholic baptism of a child: Archives of the Archdiocese of Santa Fe, Book 69-1832-33, Book 69A-1833-39. Microfilm Reel 6. William and Mary Donoho are also nonentities in the many book indexes examined from Santa Fe Trail bibliographies and other reference lists, including: Jack Rittenhouse, *The Santa Fe Trail A Historical Bibliography* (Albuquerque: University Press, 1971; facsimile rpt., Jack D. Rittenhouse, 1986); Marc Simmons, "Women on the Santa Fe Trail: Diaries, Journals, Memoirs: An Annotated Bibliography," *New Mexico Historical Review* 61 (1986): 233-43; Henry R. Wagner and Charles L. Camp, *The Plains & the Rockies: A Critical Bibliography of Exploration, Adventure and Travel in the American West, 1800-1865*, 4th ed. rev. Robert H. Becker (San Francisco: John Howell Books, 1982).

2. Spanish Archives of New Mexico I, No. 1316, Reel 6, Frames 1239-1240, NMSRCA.

3. R. L. Duffus, *The Santa Fe Trail* (Albuquerque: University of New Mexico Press, 1972), 156.

4. Josiah Gregg, *Commerce of the Prairies: or the Journal of a Santa Fe Trader, during Eight Expeditions across the Great Western Prairies, and a Residence of nearly Nine Years in Northern Mexico*, 2 vols. (New York: Henry G. Langley, 1844); rpt. ed., ed. Milo Milton Quaife (Lincoln/London: University of Nebraska Press, 1967), 140.

5. Ralph Emerson Twitchell, *Old Santa Fe, The Story of New Mexico's Ancient Capital* (Santa Fe: Santa Fe New Mexican Publishing Corporation, 1925), 228.

6. Duffus, *The Santa Fe Trail*, 157.

7. Gregg, *Commerce of the Prairies*, 102.

8. W.H.H. Allison, "Santa Fe as it Appeared During the Winter of the Years 1837 and 1838," *Old Santa Fe* 2 (1914): 176-77.

9. Matthew C. Field, "Tourist in Santa Fe, 1840," *El Palacio* 67, 1 (February 1959): 26.

10. Allison, *Old Santa Fe*, 178.

11. Ibid, 177-78.

12. Duffus, *The Santa Fe Trail*, 161-62.

13. Robert Glass Cleland, *This Reckless Breed of Men* (New York: Alfred A. Knopf, 1950), 151.

14. Susan Shelby Magoffin, *Down the Santa Fe Trail and Into Mexico, The Diary of Susan Shelby Magoffin, 1846-1847*, ed. Stella M. Drumm (New Haven: Yale University Press, 1926; rpt. ed., Lincoln: University of Nebraska Press, 1982) 115, 130-31.

15. Duffus, *The Santa Fe Trail*, 167.

16. Fray Angelico Chavez, "Dona Tules, Her Fame and Her Funeral," *El Palacio* 57, 8 (August 1950): 27-34.

17. Marc Simmons, "La Tules," *The Santa Fe Reporter,* 2 December 1987, 11.
18. Interview with Ramona Baca Latimer, Santa Fe, August 1989. Latimer, age ninety-nine in 1989, recalls that when she was about eleven years old, she and a schoolmate were on their way home from school. As they passed St. Francis Cathedral, some caskets were being exhumed and moved from the grounds of the old Parroquia. Evidently rumor flew that one was the coffin of Dona Tules and spectators gathered. Latimer remembers that she and her friend were close enough to look at Tules and her hair was indeed red. Local tradition says that Tules' burial was moved to the old San Miguel Cemetery which is now the parking lot of the PERA Building.
19. Twitchell, *Old Santa Fe,* 236; *Old Santa Fe Today,* 3rd ed. (Albuquerque: University of New Mexico Press, Historic Santa Fe Foundation, 1982), 99.
20. Rebecca McDowell Craver, *The Impact of Intimacy, Mexican-Anglo Intermarriage in New Mexico, 1821-1846* (El Paso: Texas Western Press, The University of Texas at El Paso, 1982), 59.
21. Bright Ray, *Legends of the Red River Valley* (San Antonio: The Naylor Company, 1941), 200.
22. Letter, Charles Blumner to his mother, Johanna, 3 April 1838, Folder 3, Brandt Collection, History Library, Museum of New Mexico.
23. Letter, Charles Blumner to his sister, Hannchen, 18 March 1841, Folder 3, Brandt Collection, History Library, Museum of New Mexico.
24. Janet Lecompte, *Rebellion in Rio Arriba, 1837* (Albuquerque: University of New Mexico Press, 1985), 33-34.
25. Carl Coke Rister, *Comanche Bondage, Dr. John Charles Beale's settlement of La Villa de Dolores on Las Moras Creek in Southern Texas of the 1830's with an annotated reprint of Sarah Ann Horn's Narrative of her captivity among the Comanches her ransom by traders in New Mexico and return via the Santa Fe Trail,* (Glendale: The Arthur H. Clark Company, 1955), 172.
26. John Henry Brown, *Indian Wars and Pioneers of Texas,* (Austin: L. E. Daniell, 189?) 36.
27. Spanish Archives of New Mexico I, No. 1316, NMSRCA.

Chapter Five — *The Old Fonda*

1. *Peter Hertzog, La Fonda — The Inn of Santa Fe,* (Santa Fe: The Press of the Territorian, 1962), 3.
2. John Sherman, *Santa Fe: A Pictorial History,* (Norfolk/Virginia Beach, Virginia: Donning Company, 1983), 128.
3. Urrutia, Joseph d', Map, "Planto de la Villa de Santa Fe, Capital de Nueva Mexico, 1766," New Mexico State Records Center and Archives (NMSRCA).
4. Spanish Archives of New Mexico, Twitchell I, No. 1314, NMSRCA.
5. Ralph Emerson Twitchell, *The Leading Facts of New Mexican History* (Albuquerque: Horn and Wallace, 1963), Vol. II, 138.

6. Ralph Emerson Twitchell, *Old Santa Fe, The Story of New Mexico's Ancient Capital* (Santa Fe: Santa Fe New Mexican Publishing Corporation, 1925), 237; n. 481.

7. Susan Shelby Magoffin, *Down the Santa Fe Trail and Into Mexico, The Diary of Susan Shelby Magoffin, 1846-1847*, ed. Stella M. Drumm (New Haven: Yale University Press, 1926; rpt. ed., Lincoln: University of Nebraska Press, 1982), 103.

8. Deed Records, Santa Fe County Courthouse, Book P-1, 461. For many years before its demolition, this dwelling was referred to as ''The Magoffin House,'' even though Susan and Samuel did not own it and lived there only thirty-two days. Photographs of the house after it was remodeled by the Fiskes in the 1890s were even labeled ''Magoffin House'' in the Museum of New Mexico Photo Archives. So whether it was fact or fiction, the story has been perpetuated.

9. Letter, William S. Messervy to John M. Kingsbury, 15 October 1855, Webb Collection, Missouri Historical Society, Division of Library and Archives, St Louis, Missouri.

10. Letter, Donoho to Brown, 5 February 1887.

11. Deed Records, Book A, 153-154.

12. Ibid, 155.

13. W.H.H. Allison, ''Santa Fe as it Appeared During the Winter of the Years 1837 and 1838,'' *Old Santa Fe* 2(1914): 178-79.

14. Ibid, 178.

15. Ruth Laughlin, *The Wind Leaves No Shadow* (1948; rpt. ed., Caldwell, Idaho: The Caxton Printers, Ltd., 1978), 141.

Chapter Six — *Captives of the Comanches*

1. *A Narrative of the Captivity of Mrs. Horn, and Her Two Children With Mrs. Harris, by the Camanche Indians, After They Had Murdered Their Husbands and Travelling Companions; With a Brief Account of that Nation of Savages, of Whom So Little is Generally Known* (St. Louis: C. Keemle, Printer, 1839). This edition became very rare. The 1853, or second, edition, the only one with a picture of Mrs. Horn, was titled *An Authentic and Thrilling Narrative of the Captivity of Mrs. Horn, and Her Two Children, With Mrs. Harris, by the Camanche Indians, and the Murder of Their Husbands and Traveling Companions* (Cincinnati: Published by the Author, 1853).

2. Carl Coke Rister, *Comanche Bondage, Dr. John Charles Beale's settlement of La Villa de Dolores on Las Moras Creek in Southern Texas of the 1830's with an annotated reprint of Sarah Ann Horn's Narrative of her captivity among the Comanches her ransom by traders in New Mexico and return via the Santa Fe Trail* (Glendale: The Arthur H. Clark Company, 1955), 15.

3. Ibid, 148-49.

4. John Henry Brown, *Indian Wars and Pioneers of Texas,* (Austin: L. E. Daniell, 189?), 30.

5. Ibid, 32.

6. Rister, *Comanche Bondage,* 150-53.

7. Ibid, 158-59.

8. Ibid, 179-80.

9. Ibid, 185.

10. Tommie Pinkard, "Telling of the Tales," *Texas Highways,* March 1978, 13. Today the descendants of Comanches from Oklahoma and Anglos from Texas gather annually to renew bonds of kinship in the Parker family. Using a script written by Jack Selden of Palestine, Texas, they perpetuate their history at reunions held alternately in Oklahoma or at Old Fort Parker in Texas (Tommie Pinkard, "They Come In Peace, *Texas Highways,* October 1983, 42). At the family reunions, members present story tellings about blue-eyed Cynthia Parker who was returned to her white relations after spending twenty-four years with the Comanches. She died at age thirty-seven, some said of heartbreak, torn between the two cultures.

11. Pamphlet, Old Fort Parker State Historic Site, Groesbeck, Texas, 1987.

12. Old Fort Parker State Historic Site is located between the towns of Groesbeck and Mexia, Texas. It is an authentic restoration of the original fort built in 1833.

13. Henry R. Wagner and Charles L. Camp, *The Plains and the Rockies: A Critical Bibliography of Exploration, Adventure and Travel in the American West, 1800-1865,* 4th ed. rev. Robert H. Becker (San Francisco: John Howell Books, 1982), 177. A footnote accompanying the entry on Rachael Plummer gives a good explanation of the chronology of the Rachael Plummer books: "The second edition of Mrs. Plummer's story appeared in 1844 as Part II of the *Narrative of the Perilous Adventures, . . . of Rev. James W. Parker.* The Reverend Parker was Mrs. Plummer's father, and it was through his book that her ordeal became well-known. Mrs. Plummer's preface to her part of the book states: 'In my preface to the first edition of this narrative I promised a second edition, should the first meet with public patronage.' However, until recently no copy of that first edition was known to exist. Thomas W. Streeter, in his *Bibliography of Texas* (Cambridge: Harvard University Press, 1960), number 242, was able to describe this edition only from conjecture, but correctly pointed to Houston in 1838 as the place and date of publication. Streeter also quoted from a letter of the Reverend Parker to Mirabeau Lamar, President of the Texas Republic, verifying that Mrs. Plummer was the author not only of the second narrative, published posthumously, but also of an earlier, shorter version which had been printed in her lifetime.

"It has remained for the vigilance and good fortune of Texas bookseller John Jenkins to bring to light in 1975 a copy of the long sought first edition, which is now in the Beineke Library at Yale. This little pamphlet has been reprinted in photographic facsimile in 400 copies (Austin: Jenkins Publishing Company, 1977), with a preface by Archibald Hanna and introductory essay by William Reese.''

14. Wagner and Camp list *James Parker's Narrative* in three parts: [title, Part I] *Narrative of the Perilous Adventures, Miraculous Escapes and Sufferings of Rev. James W. Parker, During a Frontier Residence in Texas, of Fifteen Years: With an Impartial Geographical Description of the Climate, Soil, Timber, Water, &C.; &C.; ,&C. of Texas; Written by Himself. To Which is Appended a Narrative of the Capture and Subsequent Sufferings of Mrs. Rachel Plummer, (His Daughter,) During a Captivity of Twenty-One Months Among the Cumanche Indians: Written by Herself.* Printed at the Morning Courier Office, 4th Street, Louisville, Ky. 1844. [title, Part II] *Narrative of the Capture and Subsequent Sufferings of Mrs. Rachel Plummer, During a Captivity of Twenty-one Months Among the Cumanche Indians: With a Sketch of Their Manners, Customs, Laws, &C., &C, With a Short Description of the Country Over Which She Travelled Whilst With the Indians. Written by Herself, 1839.* [wrapper title] *Parker's Narrative and History of Texas; to Which is Appended Mrs. Plummer's Narrative of Her Captivity of Twenty-one Months Among the Comanche Indians. "Entered According to Act of Congress, In the Year of our Lord, 1844, By James W. Parker, In the Clerk's Office Of the District Court of the State of Kentucky."* Louisville, Kentucky, 1845 (The Plains and the Rockies, 241-42):

   Wagner and Camp do not list the 1926 third edition published by Plummer descendants: *The Rachel Plummer Narrative* (n.p.: Rachel Lofton, Susie Hendrix and Jane Kennedy, 1926). Lofton and Hendrix were granddaughters and Kennedy was a great-granddaughter of Rachael Plummer. In it the name is spelled Rachel. The book is evidently a reprint of the 1844 edition, but changes were made. An inter-library loan copy of the 1844 edition was not available, but a copy of the 1926 edition was found at Corpus Christi State University in Texas. In the 1926 edition the James Parker section does not contain a Chapter I. It begins with a foreword on page 3 by the Plummer descendants. Chapter II begins on page 5 and does not have a title page for James Parker's narrative. Rachael Parker's section is titled, *Narrative of the Capture and Subsequent Sufferings of Mrs. Rachel Plummer, During a Captivity of Twenty-one Months Among the Comanche Indians; With a Sketch of Their Manners, Customs, Laws, &c., & With A Short Description of the County Over Which She Traveled Whilst With the Indian, By Herself.* (Hereafter referred to as *The Narrative of Rachel Plummer,* 1926.)

15. *Rachael Plummer's Narrative of Twenty-one Months Servitude As a Prisoner Among the Commanchee Indians,* rpt. from the 1838 original, ed. William Reese (Austin: Jenkins Publishing Company, 1977). (Hereafter referred to as *Rachael Plummer's Narrative,* 1838.) Reese also spells Rachael's name ''Rachel,'' even though the title on the book he is writing about is spelled ''Rachael.''

After Rachael's book was published in Houston in 1838, in the East two fictionalized accounts capitalized on her ordeal and the Horn-Harris story, with the women's names changed to Caroline Harris and Clarissa Plummer. William Streeter considered both stories to be fictitious but judged the Rachel Plummer and Sarah Horn narratives to be clearly authentic (Wagner and Camp, *The Plains and the Rockies*, 171). These fictional accounts had even lengthier titles than their genuine counterparts: *Caroline Harris, History of the Captivity and Providential Release Therefrom of Mrs. Caroline Harris, Wife of the late Mr. Richard Harris, of Franklin County, State of New York; Who, With Mrs. Clarissa Plumber, Wife of Mr. James Plummer, Were, in the Spring of 1835 (With Their Unfortunate Husbands,) Taken Prisoners by the Camanche Tribe of Indians, While Emigrating From Said Franklin County (N.Y.) To Texas: And After Having Been Made to Witness the Tragical Deaths of Their Husbands, and Held Nearly Two Years in Bondage, Were Providentially Redeemed Therefrom by Two of Their Countrymen Attached to a Company of Santa Fe Traders. It Was the Misfortune of Mrs. Harris, and Her Unfortunate Female Companion (Soon After the Deaths of Their Husbands,) To Be Separated by, and Compelled to Become Companions of, and to Cohabit With, Two Disgusting Indian Chiefs, and From Whom They Received the Most Cruel and Beastly Treatment* (New York: Perry and Cooke, Publishers. 1838) (Wagner and Camp, *The Plains and the Rockies*, 170). The title *Clarissa Plummer* heads the second account: *Narrative of the Captivity and Extreme Sufferings of Mrs. Clarissa Plummer, wife of the Late Mr. James Plummer, of Franklin County, State of New York; Who Was With Mrs. Caroline Harris, Wife of the Late Mr. Richard Harris, Were in the Spring of 1835, With Their Unfortunate Families, Surprised and Taken Prisoners by a Party of the Camanche Tribe of Indians, While emigrating from Said Franklin County (N. Y.) to Texas; and After Having Been Held Nearly Two Years in Captivity, and Witnessed the Deaths of their Husbands, Were Fortunately Redeemed From the Hands of the Savages by an American Fur Trader; A Native of Georgia. Mrs. Plummer Was Made Prisoner and Held in Bondage at the Same Time With the Unfortunate Mrs. Harris, With Whose Narrative the Public Have Recently Been Presented* (New York: Perry and Cooke, Publishers, 1838) (Wagner and Camp, *The Plains and the Rockies*, 176, 177). In these fictionalized versions, William Reese suggests that "the New York publishers lifted not only the basic story but many details and phrases as well from the Texas story." The 1844 edition, which Reese says is always found bound with the *James Parker Narrative*, smoothed over the horror of Rachael's original story, while the fictional accounts sensationalized her sufferings.

Interestingly, a more recent fictionalized account of Rachael's story has been written by a family descendant, Zula Plummer, *The Search for Rachel* (n. p., 1976). In it Rachael is delivered by Mexican traders to the Donohos, whose residence in Santa Fe is depicted as a "pleasant white board house with huge white columns." Mrs. Donoho is described as "plump, with wavy, nearly white hair" (50).

16. *Rachael Plummer's Narrative*, 1838, 7-9.
17. Ibid, 10.
18. *The Rachel Plummer Narrative*, 1926, 97.
19. *Rachael Plummer's Narrative*, 1838, 10.
20. Ibid, 11.
21. Ibid, 14-15.
22. *The Rachel Plummer Narrative*, 1926, 116.
23. Letter, Donoho to Brown, 5 February 1887.
24. *The Rachel Plummer Narrative*, 1926, 116.

Chapter Seven — *Return to Missouri*

1. Letter, Donoho to Brown, 5 February 1887.
2. *The Rachael Plummer Narrative*, 1926, 117.
3. *Telegraph and Texas Register*, Houston, 20 January 1838, 3.
4. John Henry Brown, *Indian Wars and Pioneers of Texas* (Austin: L. E. Daniell, 189?), 36.
5. Ibid, 37.
6. *Rachael Plummer's Narrative*, 1838, 15.
7. Ibid, 16.
8. *Telegraph and Texas Register*, Houston, 3 March 1838, 2.
9. *Rachael Plummer's Narrative*, 1838, Preface.
10. *The Rachel Plummer Narrative*, 1926, Preface.
11. *Rachel Plummer Narrative*, 1926, 28; *Rachael Plummer's Narrative*, 1838. In his introduction to the latter, editor William Reese says that life held no "chains" for Rachael, instead of "charms," as is used in James Parker's narrative.
12. *Rachel Plummer Narrative*, 1926, 31, 32.
13. The State of Texas, *Journals of the Senate*, 29 November 1850, 63.
14. Carl Coke Rister, *Comanche Bondage Dr. John Charles Beale's settlement of La Villa de Dolores on Las Moras Creek in Southern Texas of the 1830's with an annotated reprint of Sarah Ann Horn's Narrative of her captivity among the Comanches her ransom by traders in New Mexico and return via the Santa Fe Trail* (Glendale, California: The Arthur H. Clark Company, 1955), 186-87.
15. Letter, Donoho to Brown, 5 February 1887.
16. Ibid. In James' letter to Brown, he mistakenly states: "Mrs. Horn was left with some friends in Mo. until after the return of my father the second time, when she came also to the home of my grandmother where she saw my father for the first time and remained several months. While she was there at my grandmother's with my mother, my father left for Texas with Mrs. Plummer, whom he restored to her family." Donoho had escorted Rachael Plummer to Texas in February while Mrs. Horn was still in New Mexico, and obviously he had arranged with other traders for Mrs. Horn's care before he left New Mexico to take his family and the other two captives to Missouri.

17. Brown, *Indian Wars and Pioneers of Texas*, 36.
18. Probate Records, Pulaski County, Waynesville, Missouri, Book AB, 94. It is interesting to note here that the Pulaski County Courthouse burned in 1903. Most of the records were destroyed except for those in a safe in the probate judge's office. The Dodson probate document was one of those (Tom and Thurman Turpin, *Our Ancestors in Pulaski County, Missouri*, [Jefferson City: Compiled and Published by Tom and Thurman Turpin, n.d.], i).
19. Letter, Donoho to Brown, 5 February 1887.

Chapter Eight — *William and Clarksville*

1. Bright Ray, *Legends of the Red River Valley* (San Antonio: The Naylor Company, 1941), 200-201.
2. Larry Beachum, *William Becknell, Father of the Santa Fe Trade* (El Paso: Texas Western Press, 1982), 54.
3. *The Clarksville News*, 1 June 1899, 1. Files of Mary Hauser, Clarksville, Texas.
4. Ibid. Pinkie Washington was a granddaughter of Mary Donoho and the daughter of Mary Ann Donoho Ragin Cornelius and W. O. Cornelius.
5. Deed Records, 1840-1845, Red River County Courthouse, Clarksville, Texas.
6. Gifford White, *1840 Citizens of Texas*, Vol. II (Austin: n.p., 1984), ix, x, 142.
7. Deed Records, Red River County Courthouse, 9 September 1841, Book H, 128.
8. Ibid, 25 January 1840, Book C, 217.
9. Ibid, 24 February 1840, Book C, 219.
10. Ibid, 30 April 1840, Book C, 267; 4 August 1840, Book C, 359.
11. *Telegraph and Texas Register*, 17 February 1841, 3.
12. See letters between Amos L. Beaty and Winnie Allen, Texas Historical Association, Biography File, William Donoho, University of Texas at Austin. It is possible that Donoho received compensation for rescuing each of the three women, with perhaps an extra grant for his heirs.

   In 1930 Amos Beaty, an attorney in New York City and the husband of Swan Donoho, James Donoho's oldest daughter, wrote the Texas Historical Association for information on William Donoho. Swan had died two months earlier. Beaty had heard erroneously that John Henry Brown's *History of Texas* told that William Donoho had helped rescue Cynthia Ann Parker from the Indians and had received a grant of land for the action; Amos L. Beaty to Texas Historical Association, 3 October 1930. The letter was passed along to an archivist, Winnie Allen, at the University of Texas, who researched the subject. She wrote Beaty that it could not have been Cynthia Ann Parker because that rescue did not occur until 1860, after William Donoho had died. In 1930 the Brown histories had not yet been indexed, so Allen did not find the entries concerning Rachael Plummer, Sarah Horn and Mrs. Harris (Allen to Beaty, 25 October 1930). However, she did tell him that Donoho had been given three other grants of land which included: No. 254 — l league, l labor (Sabine County) p. 133; No. 5016 — l league, Headright, 12 December 1840, Cass County, p. 136; (No number) "Lost Book of Harris County," 1/3 league, Limestone County, p. 137; Winnie Allen to Beaty, 25 October 1930.

In a subsequent letter Allen wrote Beaty that she had located the grant he had asked about in Montague County (Allen to Beaty, 19 November 1930). This particular grant is listed in the *Laws of the State of Texas* and is for "a certificate for one league and labor of land [slightly over 4500 acres] to the heirs of William Donoho, deceased," dated 28 November 1850 (H. P. N. Gammel, *Laws of Texas 1822-1897*, [Austin: The Gammel Book Company, 1898], Vol. III, 837). No further correspondence was found, and since his wife was dead, it must be assumed that Beaty was simply acting out of curiosity in his quest for information.

13. Deed Records, Red River County Courthouse, 22 May 1843, Book D, 358.
14. *Standard*, 17 June 1881, 3.
15. Historical Marker, Clarksville Town Square.
16. Pat B. Clark, *The History of Clarksville and Old Red River County* (Dallas: Mathus, Van Nort & Company, 1937), 203-205.
17. Gifford White, *First Settlers of Red River County* (Austin: From originals in the General Land Office, 1981), 9-11.
18. *Standard*, 29 August 1842, 3.
19. Ibid, 24 December 1842, 3.
20. Ibid, 20 February 1845, 2.
21. Ibid, 14 June 1845, 3.
22. Ibid, 12 November 1845, 3.
23. John Henry Brown, *History of Texas From 1685 to 1892*, Vol. 1 (St. Louis: L. E. Daniell, n.d.), 259.

Chapter Nine — *Mary*

1. Probate Records, Red River County, Clarksville, Texas, 31 December 1845, Book B, 154-155.
2. *Northern Standard*, Clarksville, Texas, 7 January 1846, 3.
3. Sale Statement, William Donoho Estate Papers, Red River County Probate Records, Clarksville County Courthouse, 27 January 1846.
4. Probate Court, March Term 1847, Book E, 231.
5. Probate Records, 29 November 1848, Book E, Probate Minutes.
6. Walter Prescott Webb, ed., *The Handbook of Texas*, Vol. I (Austin: The Texas State Historical Association, 1952), 358.
7. *Northern Standard*, 10 September 1842, 3.
8. *Handbook of Texas*, Vol. I, 358.
9. *Northern Standard*, 28 September 1843, 1. In 1843 Colonel Jacob Snively received a commission from Texas to intercept Mexican caravans on the Santa Fe Trail. After several weeks of inaction, many of the men returned home to Texas. Ragin's report to the *Standard* was critical of the expedition.

10. U. S. Census, 1860, Red River County, 124.

11. Probate Records, Book F, 27-28.

12. Ibid, 25-40.

13. Deed Records, Book I, 317.

14. Ibid, Book I, 330.

15. *Marriage Records Red River County, Texas, 1845-1881* (Mesquite, Texas: Mesquite Historical and Genealogical Society, n.d.), 37.

16. U. S. Census, 1860, Slave Schedule, Red River County, Clarksville, 11-12.

17. Ibid, 35.

18. Evelyn Oppenheimer and Eugene Bowers, *Red River Dust* (Austin: Eakin Press, 1968), 39.

19. *Standard*, 2 September 1881, 3.

20. U. S. Census, 1870, Clarksville, 58

21. *Clarksville News*, 1 June 1899, 1.

22. *Standard*, 12 July 1856, 2.

23. Bright Ray, *Legends of the Red River Valley*, (San Antonio: The Naylor Company, 1941), 201.

24. *Standard*, 8 March 1856, 3; 28 August 1858, 2; 5 July 1856, 2.

25. Eugene Bowers, *The Daguerreotypist*, Unpublished manuscript, Files of Anne Evetts, Clarksville, Texas.

26. *Standard*, 3 May 1856, 2.

27. Ibid, 15 December 1855, 3.

28. Ibid, 2 August 1856, 2.

29. Ibid, 1 November 1856, 2.

30. Ibid, 21 February 1857, 2.

31. *Marriage Records*, 10.

32. *Standard*, 11 June 1859, 2.

33. Ibid, 7 March 1858, 3.

34. *Marriage Records*, 12.

35. Paul J. Hamilton, "Early History of Pulaski County" (*Pulaski County Democrat*, 20 February 1964), whose account reads: "After settling on Wet Glaize Creek [Camden County, Missouri] Dr. William M. Dodson . . . practiced over a territory that extended as far as Waynesville and Lebanon. He was also a preacher in the Methodist Episcopal Church, South, and at the time of the conflict between the states was chaplain of a Missouri regiment, serving under General Burbage." Dodson's daughter Lucie "had fled from Camden County." No reason is given, but undoubtedly it had to do with southern sympathies. She was engaged to Dr. John W. Armstrong, also a Methodist Episcopal minister, and an officer of the Confederacy.

36. Neva Crane, "The Dodson Family," *Camden County Historian* (Linn Creek, Missouri: Camden County Historical Society, 1982-83), 22.

37. *Standard*, 13 September 1862, 1.

38. *History of Laclede, Camden, Dallas, Webster, Wright, Texas, Pulaski, Phelps,*

and Dent Counties, Missouri (Chicago: Goodspeed Publishing Company, 1889), 890.

39. *Standard*, 24 October 1857, 3.
40. U. S. Census, 1860, Clarksville, 124.
41. *Standard*, 15 May 1858, 2.
42. Ibid, 19 December 1847, 2; 1 December 1855, 3.
43. Newspaper clipping, 31 May 1872. Newspaper unknown. It did not appear in the *Standard*. No obituary for Mary Ann was found during research on the book. During the final editing, this was found in the family papers by Elma McWhorter and sent, with other ephemera, to the author.
44. *Standard*, 22 June 1861, 2.
45. Files of Mary Hauser, Clarksville.
46. Ray, *Legends of the Red River Valley*, 202.
47. Ibid, 209.
48. U. S. Census, 1880, Clarksville, 24.
49. Letter, Mary Kate Hale to Marian Meyer, 21 May 1987, Meyer Files.
50. U. S. Census, 1870, Clarksville, 8.
51. *Standard*, 16 January 1880, 3.
52. Probate Records, Will of Mary Donoho, Book K, 101.
53. Ibid, 98.
54. Ibid, 97.
55. Ibid, 96, 98.
56. The remainder of the list of hotel furnishings is a fascinating document, considered in the context of today's prices. Sixty-three quilts, which would have been handmade, were valued at one dollar each. Eight walnut washstands, which more than likely had marble tops, were priced at two dollars each. At a lesser value of one dollar apiece were ten pine washstands. Twenty-one bowl and pitcher sets which would have stood on those wash stands had a price tag of one dollar each. Any one of these items would fetch a high price in an antique store today.
57. Ibid, 162.
58. Ibid, 162-64.

Chapter Ten — *Donoho Descendants*

1. *Standard*, 1 July 1881, 3.
2. Ibid, 27 August 1880, 3.
3. Ibid, 6 October 1882, 3.
4. Ibid, 28 August 1885, 3.
5. Probate Records, Will of James B. Donoho, Book Z, 123.
6. News clipping, n.d. James Donoho died 23 November 1908. This probably appeared in the *Clarksville News*, of which no known copies are extant. Shortly before the editing process on the book was complete, it was found in the family papers and sent to the author by Elma McWhorter.

7. Interview with Ruth McCulloch, 1 June 1987, Clarksville.

8. Albert Nelson Marquis, *Who's Who in America*, 1922-1923, Vol. 12 (Chicago: The A. N. Marquis Company, 1938), 337.

9. Ibid, Vol. 20, 1938-1939, 278.

10. Letter, Pat C. Beadle, Attorney-at-Law, Clarksville, to Marian Meyer, 10 March 1988, Meyer File.

11. Ibid. Attached to the letter from Beadle is a Certificate of Cremation for Mattie Bayless, Graceland Cemetery Company, Evanston, Illinois.

12. *Red River County Texas Cemeteries*, Vol. 1 (Clarksville: Bertha L. Gable, 1984), 55.

13. Letter, Caryl S. Scott, Scott & Hebblethwaite Funeral Home, Glenview, Illinois, to Meyer, 9 May 1988, Meyer File.

14. Probate Records, Will of Mary Pearson, Book 31, 297-300.

15. Letter, Elma Cornelius McWhorter, Palestine, Texas, to Meyer, 24 June 1988, Meyer File.

16. Probate Records, Will of Mary Pearson, Book 31, 297-300.

17. *Standard*, 9 June 1882, 3.

18. Letters, Will Cornelius to Imogene Kibbe, 23 July 1891, and n.d. All Cornelius letters and ephemera are in the McWhorter file.

19. Ibid, 16 August 1981.

20. *Gainesville Daily Register*, 29 December 1891, 1.

21. Letter, Will Cornelius to Imogene Cornelius, 14 January 1893.

22. Receipt, to Will and Imogene Cornelius from Zue Cornelius, 28 March 1905. Zue was one of Captain Cornelius' children from his subsequent marriage after Mary Ann Cornelius died in 1872.

23. Report Card, Boscobel College, Nashville, Tennessee, 1910-1911.

24. Letter, Cammie Cornelius to her parents, 28 November 1913.

25. Letter, Cammie Cornelius to Will Cornelius, 7 March 1912.

26. Letter, Cammie Cornelius to Raymond Cornelius, Sr., n.d., circa 1965, Cornelius file. The picture referred to was undoubtedly the portrait of Mary Donoho which burned in the hotel fire.

27. Interview with Raymond E. Cornelius, Jr., 11 July 1988, Palestine, Texas.

Bibliography

ARCHIVAL MATERIALS

Eugene Barker Texas History Center, University of Texas, Austin: John Henry Brown Papers, 1691-1951. Biography File.

National Archives, Washington, D. C. Record Group 94, AGO Letters Rec.

New Mexico State Records Center and Archives, Santa Fe: Manuel Alvarez Papers, Mexican Archives of New Mexico, Spanish Archives of New Mexico, Maps.

Joint Collection University of Missouri Western Historical Manuscript Collection-State Historical Society of Missouri, Manuscripts, Columbia: Ramsey Place Names Collection No. 2366.

Missouri Historical Society, Division of Library and Archives, St. Louis, Missouri: Webb Collection.

Museum of New Mexico History Library, Santa Fe: Brandt Collection.

Pulaski County Courthouse, Waynesville, Missouri: Probate Records.

Red River County Courthouse, Clarksville, Texas: Deed Records, Probate Records.

Santa Fe County Courthouse, Santa Fe: Deed Records.

United States Census Records: New Mexico Territory: 1850, 1860, 1870, 1880, Texas: Red River County, 1850, 1860, 1870, 1880. Red River County, Slave Schedule, 1860.

NEWSPAPERS

Clarksville News, Texas
Missouri Intelligencer, Columbia
Northern Standard, later the *Standard*, Clarksville, Texas
Pulaski County Democrat, Waynesville, Missouri
The Reveille, Linn Creek, Missouri
Santa Fe New Mexican
Santa Fe Republican, New Mexico
Telegraph and Texas Register, Houston

UNPUBLISHED SOURCES

Bork, Albert William. *Nuevos Aspectos del Comercio entre Nueve Mexico y Misuri, 1822-46*. Mexico: Thesis Kue Presenta, Albert William Bork, Para Obtener El Grado de Doctor en Letras. Mexico 1944. Coronado

Microfilm HF 3155 B64, Center for Southwest Research Studies, University of New Mexico, General Library, Special Collections.

PERSONAL FILES

Anne Evetts, Clarksville, Texas
  Bowers, Eugene. *The Daguerrotypist*, n.d.
Raymond E. Cornelius, Jr., Lufkin, Texas
Mary Hauser, Clarksville, Texas
Marian Meyer, Santa Fe, New Mexico
Elma McWhorter, Palestine, Texas

PERSONAL INTERVIEWS

Ruth McCulloch, Clarksville, Texas, 1 June 1987
Ramona Latimer, Santa Fe, New Mexico, 26 July 1988
Elma McWhorter, Palestine, Texas, 11 July 1988
Raymond Cornelius, Palestine, Texas, 11 July 1988
Keith McCann, Camdenton, Missouri, 12 July 1989

SECONDARY SOURCES

Allison, W.H.H. "Santa Fe As It Appeared in the Winter of 1837-38" *Old Santa Fe 2* (1914), 170-83.

Barry, Louise. *The Beginning of the West*. Topeka: Kansas State Historical Society, 1972.

Beachum, Larry. *William Becknell: Father of the Santa Fe Trail*. El Paso: Texas Western Press, 1982.

Bieber, Ralph Paul. *The Papers of James J. Webb, Santa Fe Merchant, 1844-1861*. Reprint, Washington University Studies, Vol XI, Hanamistic Series, No. 2, 1924. 255-305.

Brown, John Henry. *History of Texas From 1685 to 1892*. 2 Vols. St. Louis: L.E. Daniell, 1892.

———. *Indian Wars and Pioneers of Texas*. Austin: L. E. Daniell, 189?.

Burroughs, Jean M. *Bride of the Santa Fe Trail*. Santa Fe: Sunstone Press, 1984.

Chacon, Rafael. *Legacy of Honor*. Edited by Jacqueline Dorgan Meketa. Albuquerque: University of New Mexico Press, 1986.

Chavez, Fray Angelico. "Dona Tules, Her Fame and Her Funeral." *El Palacio* 57, 8 (August 1950): 227-34.

Clark, Pat B. *The History of Clarksville and Old Red River County*. Dallas: Mathus, Van Nort and Company, 1937.

Cleland, Robert Glass. *This Reckless Breed of Men*. New York: Alfred A. Knopf, 1950.

Crane, Neva. *Camden County Historian*. Linn Creek, Missouri: Camden County Historical Society, 1982-83.

Craver, Rebecca McDowell. *The Impact of Intimacy: Mexican-Anglo Intermarriage in New Mexico, 1821-1846*. El Paso: Texas Western Press, The University of Texas at El Paso, 1982.

Dodson, Rev. William M. "Autobiography." *Camden County Historian*. Linn Creek, Missouri: Camden County Historical Society, 1982-83, 22-24.

Duffus, R. L. *The Santa Fe Trail*. Albuquerque: University of New Mexico Press, 1972.

Field, Matthew C. "Tourist in Santa Fe." *El Palacio 67*, 1 (February 1959): 1-15.

Gregg, Josiah. *Commerce of the Prairies*. Edited by Milo Milton Quaife. Lincoln/London: University of Nebraska Press, 1967.

Hertzog, Peter [Philip St. George Cook III]. *La Fonda: The Inn of Santa Fe*. Santa Fe: The Press of the Territorian, 1962.

History of Laclede, Camden, Dallas, Webster, Wright, Texas, Pulaski, Phelps, and Dent Counties, Missouri. Chicago: Goodspeed Publishing Company, 1889.

Hodges, Nadine and Mrs. Howard W. Woodruff. "County and Genealogical Record." *Missouri Pioneers* 21 (1973) 56-59.

Lavender, David. *Bent's Fort*. Garden City, New York: Doubleday & Company, Inc., 1954.

Laughlin, Ruth. *The Wind Leaves No Shadow*. 1948; rpt. ed. Caldwell, Idaho: The Caxton Printers, Ltd., 1978.

Laws of Fifth Legislature, The State of Texas. Austin: J. W. Hampton, State Printer, 1854.

Laws of Texas 1822-1897. Compiled by H.P.N Gammel. 3 vols. Austin: The Gammel Book Company, 1898.

Magoffin, Susan Shelby. *Down the Santa Fe Trail and into Mexico*. Edited by Stella M. Drumm. Lincoln and London: University of Nebraska Press, 1982.

Marriage Records Red River County, Texas, 1845-1881. Mesquite, Texas: Mesquite Historical and Genealogical Society, n.d.

Meyer, Marian. "They Were Alone Among the Heathen." *Santa Fe Reporter*, 28 March 1984, 13.

Moreland, Fern. "Glaize City." *Camden County Historian*. Linn Creek, Missouri: Camden County Historical Society, 1982-83, 20.

Oliva, Leo E. *Soldiers on the Santa Fe Trail*. Norman: University of Oklahoma Press, 1967.

Oppenheimer, Evelyn and Eugene Bowers. *Red River Dust*. Austin: Eakin Press, 1968.

Ormesher, Susan. *Missouri Marriages Before 1840*. Baltimore: Genealogical Publishing Company, 1982.

Pinkard, Tommie. "Telling of the Tales." *Texas Highways*, March 1978, 13-15.

————. "They Come in Peace." *Texas Highways*, October 1983, 42-47.

Plummer, Rachael. *Rachael Plummer's Narrative* (Reprint from the 1838 original). Austin: Jenkins Publishing Company, 1977.

Plummer, Rachel. *The Rachel Plummer Narrative*. (Reprint from the 1844 Edition). N.p.: Rachel Lofton, Susie Hendrix and Jane Kennedy, 1926.

Plummer, Zula. *The Search for Rachel*. N.p., 1976.

Ray, Bright. *Legends of the Red River Valley*. San Antonio: The Naylor Company, 1941.

Rister, Carl Coke. *Comanche Bondage, Dr. John Charles Beale's Settlement of La Villa de Dolores on Las Moras Creek in Southern Texas of the 1830's with an annotated reprint of Sarah Ann Horn's Narrative of her Captivity among the Comanches her ransom by traders in New Mexico and return via the Santa Fe Trail*. Glendale, California: The Arthur H. Clark Company, 1955.

Rittenhouse, Jack D. *The Santa Fe Trail: A Historical Bibliography*. Albuquerque: University Press, 1971. Facsimile ed. Albuquerque: Jack D. Rittenhouse, 1986.

Russell, Marian Sloan. *Land of Enchantment, Memoirs of Marian Russell Along the Santa Fe Trail, As dictated to Mrs. Hal Russell*. Albuquerque: University of New Mexico Press, 1981.

Sherman, John. *Santa Fe: A Pictorial History*. Norfolk/Virginia Beach, Virginia: Donning Company, 1983.

Simmons, Marc. "La Tules." *Santa Fe Reporter*. 2 December 1987, 10.

————. "New Mexico's Spanish Exiles." *New Mexico Historical Review*, 59 (1984): 67-79.

————. "Women on the Santa Fe Trail: Diaries, Journals, Memoirs. An Annotated Bibliography." *New Mexico Historical Review* 61 (1986): 233-43.

Turpin, Tom and Thurman. *Our Ancestors in Pulaski County, Missouri*. Jefferson City: Tom and Thurman Turpin, n.d.

Twitchell, Ralph Emerson. *The Leading Facts of New Mexican History*. 1911-17. Facsimile ed. 2 vols. Albuquerque: Horn and Wallace, 1963.

_____. *Old Santa Fe: The Story of New Mexico's Ancient Capital*. Santa Fe: Santa Fe New Mexican Publishing Corporation, 1925.

Wagner, Henry R. and Charles L. Camp. *The Plains & the Rockies: A Critical Bibliography of Exploration, Adventure and Travel in the American West, 1800-1865*. 4th ed. rev. Robert H. Becker. San Francisco: John Howell Books, 1982.

Webb, Walter Prescott, ed. *The Handbook of Texas*. 2 Vols. Austin: The Texas State Historical Association, 1952.

Weber, David J., ed. *The Extranjeros: Selected Documents from the Mexican Side of the Santa Fe Trail*. Santa Fe: Stagecoach Press, 1967.

White, Gifford. *First Settlers of Red River County*. Austin, Texas: From Originals in General Land Office, 1981.

_____. *1840 Citizens of Texas Volume 2 Tax Rolls*. Austin, Texas: 1984.

Whitsitt, William H. *Genealogy of Jefferson Davis*. New York and Washington: The Neale Publishing Company, 1910.

Williams, Jacqueline Hogan, and Betty Harvey Williams. *Camden County Missouri Tombstone Inscriptions*. Vol. I. Warrensburg, Missouri: n.p., 1968, 61-64.

Williams, Walter. *The State of Missouri*. Columbia: Press of E. W. Stephens, 1904.

Index